Games, Lies and Politics:

Lessons in Municipal Governance, Leadership and Ethics

Charles A. Montoya

Table of Contents

Preface 1

Dedication... 3

Introduction: Why This Book, and Why Now.................................. 4

Chapter 1: The Three Ps 6

Chapter 3: Bringing People Who Add to You................................ 16

Chapter 4: Reading People, Believing in People, Trusting People.. 22

Chapter 5: The Endgame 30

Chapter 6: Why Even Have a Box.. 35

Chapter 7: Opportunity to Excel (OTE) 41

Chapter 8: Talking, Listening, Hearing 46

Chapter 9: Leading for Legacy or Last Paycheck?........................ 54

Chapter 10: Let the Other Person Always Talk First 61

Chapter 11: Enemies in the Hallway 66

Chapter 12: The Community 74

Chapter 13: Never Say No.. 84

Chapter 14: When You're Used, Abused, and Thrown to the Curb. 88

Chapter 15: Gotcha Moments.. 95

Chapter 16: The Quiet Power of Consistency 103

Chapter 17: Elected Officials Are Not Your Friends 108

Chapter 18: Why Electeds Run for Office.................................... 115

Chapter 19: National Organizations and Their Role....................... 122

Chapter 20: Support Networks, Ethics Boards, and Advocacy 128

Chapter 21: Know When It's Time to Walk Away.......................... 134

Chapter 22: The End of the Road 139

Chapter 23: The Media Friend, Foe, or Force of Nature? 143

Chapter 24: Family, Health, and the Human Side of Leadership .. 149

Chapter 25: The Paper Trail: Protect Yourself 154

Chapter 26: Reinventing yourself after Public Service 160

Epilogue: After the Title Is Gone 167

Final Thoughts: The Quiet Strength of Leadership 168

Acknowledgment 170

One Last Acknowledgment 172

Preface

I didn't write this book because everything went right in my career—
I wrote it because a lot of things went wrong.

Over the years, I've served in some of the most challenging roles in
local government: city manager, public administrator, change agent,
crisis manager, and, when necessary, the shield between staff and
political fire. I've been praised for building strong teams, navigating
through community upheaval, and cleaning up broken systems. I've
also been blamed for decisions I didn't make, attacked for standing
my ground, and asked to quietly look away when something unethical
was happening.

You can research me and find many articles good, bad, and
interesting, but as I tell people, "When they let you go, they try to
write the story line." However, I have never been indicted, found
liable for anything in my career, and not even a speeding ticket in over
35 years. So, a reminder to never believe what you read in the press—
verify.

In this field, if you do your job well, no one notices. But if you do it
with integrity, someone will eventually try to take you out.

This book is a reflection of a career spent walking that tightrope—
between leadership and survival, between progress and politics,
between protecting others and trying to protect yourself. It's not a
leadership textbook. It's not a memoir. It's a guide for those who find
themselves in the chair where the buck stops—and who are trying to
hold onto their values while still getting the job done.

You'll find stories here—some personal, some universal. You'll find
principles I've lived by and hard lessons I've had to learn, sometimes
more than once. You'll see the moments that shaped me as a leader,
and the moments that nearly broke me. And most importantly, you'll
see the decisions I had to make when no one was watching—because
in public service, those are the ones that define you.

If you're a city or county manager, a department head, a public servant, or even an elected official trying to understand the weight of the roles around you—this book is for you. It's for anyone who's been lied to, set up, pushed out, or asked to compromise their integrity for the sake of politics.

Leadership is lonely. But you're not alone.

You won't find easy answers here. What you will find is someone who's been through the fire and is still standing, and willing to say the things most people are too afraid to say out loud. This book was written with the intent for the reader to process Chapters as needed and to complete in a short period of time, rather than spending hours on each chapter.

Because public service matters. Ethics matter. And so does the way we treat the people who carry the burden of both.

— Charles A. Montoya

Dedication

To Asusena—

This book exists because of the quiet belief of one extraordinary person—and her not-so-quiet reminders to finish both this book and my career with clarity and courage.

You've helped me carry the weight of this work and reminded me again and again that I was not alone.

I dedicate these words to you, with all my love and gratitude.

— Charles

Introduction: Why This Book, and Why Now

If you're reading this, chances are you're one of three people: You're a public servant—an assistant city manager, department director, or staffer hoping to rise to the top seat in your organization; or you're an elected official, sitting at the dais, unsure of what your manager does all day—or why they won't always give you a straight yes or no; or you may be a college student in Public Administration.

I wrote this book for all of you. Because local government is a world full of contradictions: service masked by strategy, integrity tested by politics, and leadership often rewarded with silence or suspicion.

And after more than 30 years in public service, I've come to a simple conclusion: nobody tells the truth about this job—until it's too late to benefit from it.

The title is blunt. It's meant to be. We love to talk about city government as clean, objective, policy-driven. But anyone who's actually done this work knows it's far messier. There are games played behind the scenes, truths twisted into lies, and politics that can break a good manager or bend a good policy—and none of it gets mentioned during new councilmember orientation or in your MPA coursework.

This book exists to expose those truths—not to attack the system, but to equip those who have to navigate it. Because understanding the game doesn't mean you have to play dirty. But pretending the game doesn't exist? That'll get you fired.

I've served in local government leadership for more than three decades—as a city manager, assistant city manager, economic development director, consultant, Legislative and Executive Government Analyst. I hold a master's in public administration, a master's in legal studies, and I'm a graduate of the U.S. Navy Supply Corps School. This book is a distillation of those lessons.

This is not a textbook. You won't find theories on public budgeting or org charts of ideal municipal structures. What you'll find instead is a manual for surviving and thriving in the political trenches.

What you will find within these pages, you won't find in any textbook—or pretty much any other book written by another author. Because most of them haven't done this job for decades. Most of them don't understand what we go through. And most of them wouldn't survive it.

If you're serious about the work—about serving your city, protecting your team, and leading with integrity in the middle of chaos—then let's begin where every successful public servant must: With Perception. Perseverance. Patience. The Three Ps.

— Charles A. Montoya

City Manager | Consultant
Master of Public Administration
Master of Legal Studies
Graduate, U.S. Navy Supply Corps School

Chapter 1: The Three Ps

Every city manager, county administrator, or public executive will at some point face the question: *How do you survive this job while still doing it well?*

The answer lies in what I call the Three Ps—Perception, Perseverance, and Patience. These are more than just words; they're your mental survival guide, your emotional compass, and your personal and professional shield.

You won't find them on any performance review form. You won't hear them talked about during council meetings. But I promise you this: the Three Ps will determine your success, your stability, and your sanity.

Perception

Perception is not just how others see you—it's what they believe about your motives, your values, and your direction. In government, perception often outweighs truth. You might have followed every rule, dotted every "i," and still be accused of secrecy or bias. Why? Because the story people see is the one they believe.

You must manage perception like you manage your budget—with intention, precision, and clarity.

- Don't assume your silence will be interpreted as professionalism.

- Don't assume people understand the complexity behind your decisions.

- Don't assume the truth will outrun the rumor.

Control the narrative, or the narrative will control you. That doesn't mean spin. It means presence. It means transparency. It means communicating before you're asked and explaining before you're questioned.

Perseverance

Perseverance isn't about surviving one scandal or one angry meeting. It's about showing up day after day, knowing you'll be second-guessed, misunderstood, or ignored—and still choosing to lead with integrity.

This job will challenge you in ways no class or conference ever prepared you for. The Three Ps—especially perseverance—are the invisible armor that keep you upright.

When you're called names publicly…

When your staff fails you privately…

When the very people who begged you to take the job now want you out…

Perseverance is showing up anyway. It's knowing that storms pass—but only if you're still standing when they do.

And when it all starts to weigh on you—which it will—remember: your perseverance is part of your emotional integrity. It's what allows you to step back, reflect logically, and not react impulsively or destructively.

Patience

You will want to react. You will want to answer back. You will want to correct the record, confront the critic, and call out the lie. And sometimes, you'll need to. But more often, you'll need patience.

Patience to:

- Let the noise pass before you speak.

- Let the truth surface over time.

- Let people grow into understanding your decisions.

Patience is not passivity. It's strategic restraint. It's choosing the long game over the short win. And it's essential to preserving your credibility when others are losing theirs.

The Three Ps Are Your Shield

The Three Ps are not just abstract concepts. They are your shield—your daily protection as you navigate issues, people, politics, and even personal attacks. When things go wrong—and they will—Perception, Perseverance, and Patience will give you space to pause, breathe, and respond with both logic and emotional integrity.

This job doesn't just test your skills. It tests your soul. And without these core principles, the weight of the work will crush the meaning behind it.

And in all of this reading—and everything you read going forward in this book—it's important to note: the Three Ps are not just important for the reasons stated, but for your personal integrity.

Expect the Unexpected

Many of the hardest moments in this job will come from directions you never expected. Attacks will come from anyone, anywhere, anytime—even from those you thought were your strongest supporters.

You have to be prepared for everything and nothing—and that's not a contradiction. It's a mindset.

That's why I often compare this job to chess.

You don't plan one move ahead—you plan multiple moves ahead in every direction. You anticipate countermoves, distractions, hidden agendas. You play to survive, and to protect the institution, not just yourself.

When Your Standing Alone

There will be times—many times—when it gets hard and no one stands with you. No one calls. No one defends. No one cares. You'll walk into meetings with a smile while carrying the weight of private stress no one sees.

In those moments, the Three Ps become not just your tools—but your anchor.

They remind you of who you are, why you lead, and how to move through the moment without destroying your purpose—or your peace.

Leadership Without Exposure

You'll encounter situations no mentor warned you about. Unexpected politics. Shifting alliances. Budget ambushes. Legal surprises. Personal betrayals.

The most important thing you can do? Do not wear your emotions on your sleeve.

Whether you're ecstatic, angry, exhausted, or anxious—don't show it. Be the steady hand on the wheel. Let others react while you remain composed.

That doesn't mean you don't feel. It means your feelings don't drive your decisions.

Your steadiness will become your credibility. People trust leaders who don't unravel under pressure. Even when you're being tested—or targeted—show them perseverance, not panic.

The Shrinking Shelf Life

The average tenure of a city or county manager is constantly changing, becoming shorter, and dropped significantly in the last few decades—and continues to fall.

Why?

Because the field is changing. Politics are more personal. Attacks are more public. Elected officials are more confrontational. And the expectations are more contradictory.

It's not enough to be technically skilled—you must be politically savvy, emotionally resilient, and constantly self-aware.

Only those who understand the Three Ps—and live them—survive this career long enough to do lasting good.

Integrity as a Constant

All of this—everything you read in this book, everything I've lived through—comes back to this point: your principles are not just your professional compass, they are your personal shield.

The Three Ps don't just help you do the job. They help you preserve your integrity, your mental health, and your sense of self in a career that often tries to strip those away.

◆ Chapter 1 Summary

In a job where everything is public and nothing is personal to them, but "to you" - the Three Ps are your silent shield—protecting your integrity, preserving your purpose, and preparing you for the storm. Again this is your shield.

Chapter 2: Management vs. Leadership

In municipal government, the words "manager" and "leader" are often used interchangeably. But they're not the same thing.

You can be a manager by title—but that doesn't make you a leader.

And you can be a leader without ever holding a managerial title.

This distinction matters—because the gap between management and leadership is often where professional success stalls and personal burnout begins.

Management Is Structure—Leadership Is Substance

Management is about systems, processes, budgets, policies, procedures, deadlines, and compliance. These things are essential. They keep the machinery of government functioning. They allow for accountability and transparency.

But leadership?

Leadership is about people.

It's about vision, tone, communication, trust, adaptability, and influence. It's how you respond when the plan falls apart, the council turns on you, or the media misquotes you. It's not found in an org chart—it's earned through presence, consistency, and character.

Who Decides You Are a Leader?

You don't get to decide that you're the leader—other people do.

That's the biggest truth no one tells you when you enter executive service.

You can call yourself a city manager, a director, or a chief of staff. But titles don't guarantee trust, respect, or influence.

In fact, here's an exercise I use to highlight this point:

You can be a building manager, parking lot manager, or store manager—but try swapping the word "manager" with "leader."

- Building leader?

- Parking lot leader?

- Store leader?

It doesn't sound right, does it?

Because even with the word "manager" in the title, it doesn't automatically imply leadership.

Leadership isn't about what's printed on a business card—it's about how people respond to your presence, your decisions, and your values.

Even if you hold the title, it may be an empty job title.

Leadership is not claimed. It's confirmed—by those around you.

The Trap of a Title

There's danger in chasing titles. When you define your identity solely by a title, you miss the deeper opportunity to shape culture, mentor staff, and inspire trust.

Leadership is a role you grow into. Management is a title you're hired into. The two must eventually meet—or one will undermine the other.

Real-World Implications for City/County Managers

If you operate only as a manager, you'll focus solely on technical competence. You'll know every policy. You'll close every project on time. But you'll miss the nuance of governing: coalition-building, staff morale, council dynamics, community narratives.

If you lead without managing, you'll inspire—but create chaos. Teams will rally around you but fall apart from lack of structure.

You must do both—but know when to lead, and when to manage.

This balance determines how long you last in your role, and how effective you are while you're in it.

Common Misconceptions and Pitfalls

1. "Leadership means being liked."

False. Leadership means being respected. Sometimes that means disappointing people. Often it means doing what's right, not what's popular.

2. "If I do the job well, people will follow."

Not always. Leadership is not transactional—it's relational. People don't just follow competence. They follow consistency, fairness, and presence.

3. "Once I'm the manager, I've made it."

Not quite. That's when the real work starts. Titles don't shield you from scrutiny—they increase it.

Illustrative Examples

There were times in my career when I managed extremely well—budgets were balanced, grants secured, and audits clean. But the environment was cold. Staff were disengaged. Council didn't know me. The public didn't trust me.

I was managing. But I wasn't leading.

Other times, I took risks—spoke from the heart at town halls, acknowledged mistakes openly, and asked staff what they needed instead of assuming.

I saw morale rise. I saw partnerships form. I saw trust grow.

That's leadership. And it didn't come from my title. It came from being real and present.

Strategic Takeaways for Professionals

- Earn your influence before you need to use it. Don't wait until a crisis to build trust.

- Develop your leadership muscle daily. Read, reflect, and ask for feedback—even when it's hard.

- Recognize that leadership has a cost. You'll be targeted more, challenged more, and second-guessed more. But the impact is worth it.

- Balance structure with heart. Know the rules, but also know your people.

◆ Chapter 2 Summary

Titles are given. Leadership is earned. In government, you manage systems—

but you lead people. Know the difference, or the system will eventually manage you.

Chapter 3: Bringing People Who Add to You

In public service, your success as a leader depends not just on your decisions—but on the people you choose to surround yourself with.

The ones you hire, promote, keep, and trust will either elevate your leadership or quietly erode it. That's why bringing people who add to you—personally and professionally—isn't just a preference. It's a necessity.

When you're in an executive role, you are constantly pulled in multiple directions: council, staff, community, vendors, politics, emergencies, and expectations. Some people will help you carry that weight. Others will add more to your load while pretending to assist. Recognizing that difference is one of the most important skills a municipal leader can develop.

Your inner circle—both staff and colleagues—must be people who replenish your energy, not drain it. They must speak truth to you without ego. They must be willing to take ownership and share credit. When you hire or promote people based solely on their technical skills, you miss the more critical measure: Are they aligned with the mission of the organization, or yours? Are they honest? Are they quietly building your trust—or silently subtracting from it?

Identifying and Understanding Toxic People

Toxic people don't always scream or sabotage openly. Sometimes, they smile. They comply. They whisper. They sow doubt. They undercut meetings with side conversations and subtle eyerolls. They hoard information. They don't promote others' success—they quietly compete against it.

Toxicity often stems from insecurity, a need for control, or resentment over perceived slights. That doesn't make someone evil—it makes them dangerous to organizational health. And unlike external enemies, toxic individuals often come from within—sometimes even from within your trusted team.

As a leader, your job is to try and understand before you judge. Ask:

- What motivates this person?

- Can it be redirected into something healthy?

- Is this behavior correctable—or is it embedded in their character?

- Does this person reflect the tone I want my organization to model or the mission?

Sometimes, people act out because they feel unheard or unappreciated. A strong leader will attempt to educate and correct before moving to discipline. But you must also be honest with yourself: if that effort fails, and toxicity remains, you have to be ready to make the hard call – which most of the time is often unpopular.

Know When It's Time to Let Them Go

Removing someone—especially someone competent on paper—is not an easy decision. But it becomes essential when their presence corrodes the culture, chips away at morale, or causes others to withdraw and disengage.

Here's the painful truth: toxic people don't just affect you—they affect everyone around you. They poison meetings, fracture communication, and distract from mission. Your best employees will spend time dodging drama instead of pursuing purpose. Over time, good staff leave—not because they resent the work, but because they can no longer tolerate the environment.

Culture Is Like Vanilla Ice Cream

I heard this analogy somewhere a long time ago, and it makes sense.

Culture in an organization is like a bowl of vanilla ice cream. Smooth. Consistent. Dependable. Inviting.

Now imagine taking one single drop of hot sauce and putting it on top of that bowl.

Just one drop.

It doesn't matter how pure or perfect the rest of the bowl was—that one drop ruins the entire experience.

That drop is your toxic team member. That drop is the passive-aggressive whisper, the eyeroll in a staff meeting, the cold shoulder, the missed deadline followed by a half-hearted excuse. It may be small. It may go unnoticed by some. But over time, that one drop affects everything: morale, performance, trust.

As a leader, protecting culture isn't about perfection. It's about consistency and safety. It's about knowing that even one misaligned person can wreck the trust you've spent years building.

The Strength to Say Goodbye

Letting someone go doesn't mean you failed. It means you recognized a misalignment and chose the organization over your own comfort, and other people's opinions. It also means you're protecting everyone else who depends on a healthy, stable work environment.

If it's time to let someone go, always give them options—whether it's resignation, termination, or other options, but allow them the choice where possible. Dignity in departure matters. Let people leave with whatever integrity they have left. Don't compound their exit by bashing them publicly or internally. They still need to move forward somewhere else—doing so speaks to your integrity.

And remember: Only a weak manager continually blames others, whether inside the organization or in the public domain. Leadership is measured by how you act when it's hardest to stay composed.

Choosing Builders Over Drainers

I always told my boys: "Bring people into your life that add to it—not take from it."

They once asked what I meant. I told them, "There are people out there who exist solely for themselves. They'll take your energy, your confidence, and your stability—bit by bit. But if you surround yourself with people who add to your life, you'll grow. You'll become smarter, more empathetic, and a true leader—not a follower."

This advice holds true in professional life, too. As a leader, you should hire people who are smarter than you in some areas—more skilled, more dynamic, or more experienced in specific subject matters. If you're afraid of hiring someone brighter than you, you're limiting your own growth and the organization's future. Not to mention underlining your own insecurities for everyone else.

A strong manager isn't intimidated by excellence—they cultivate it.

Hiring strong, capable, innovative people allows you to:

- Continue learning from your team.

- Expand your leadership impact without micromanaging. Micromanaging is not always a bad thing, but it should be used as a condition to assist in a person's growth and mentorship. However, it is mostly used either by an insecure manager or trying to push someone out of an organization.

- Prepare the next generation of leaders and ensure succession planning for your organization.

But if you consistently hire people less capable or less visionary than you, it will show. It will affect your credibility, your oversight capacity, and ultimately, the perception of your leadership.

Know Who Energizes You

One of the most overlooked aspects of effective leadership is understanding your own energy type—and recognizing how those around you either recharge or deplete it.

Are you and Introvert or Extrovert? Know the difference.

- Introverts gain energy by being alone and feel drained after prolonged social interaction.

- Extroverts gain energy through interaction and stimulation, and may feel depleted when alone or disconnected.

Which one are you? Knowing this is critical—not just for self-care, but for hiring decisions, team dynamics, and conflict resolution.

Understanding your personality will help you:

- Anticipate how you'll feel after intense meetings or large community events.

- Structure your schedule to include strategic downtime or connection, depending on your type.

- Avoid burnout by managing your energy like you manage your time.

This awareness also helps you manage better, because you'll recognize when you're feeling overloaded or disconnected—not because of workload, but because of people dynamics. You'll learn when you need to get some air, take a break, or shift how you're working.

Understand Others—and Stay Shielded but Notice from a Distance

This recognition and identification also gives you tools to work with elected officials, especially those with opposite personality traits. It allows you to adjust your approach during sensitive or crisis moments.

You may also notice that some people temporarily change their personality traits to navigate a situation. Extroverts may go quiet under pressure; introverts may speak up in an emergency. Recognizing these shifts can help you lead with empathy and communicate more effectively.

But here's something equally important:

Even though you understand your own energy type—you don't need to advertise it.

People should not inherently know how to manipulate or react to your personal rhythm. Just like your emotions, your personality type is part of your shield. Knowing yourself is power—but broadcasting it is vulnerability. Also, understand that vulnerability is good sometimes – its authentic.

◆ Chapter 3 Summary

Leadership isn't just about what you bring to the table—it's about who sits with you.

Surround yourself with builders, release the drainers, and protect the culture like your credibility depends on it—because it does.

Remember: Bring people into your life that add to it, not take from it!

Chapter 4: Reading People, Believing in People, Trusting People

One of the hardest skills to develop in this job—and one of the most important—is learning how to read people, believe in people, and trust people. It sounds simple. But as time goes on, you'll realize it's one of the most complex balancing acts you'll ever face as a municipal executive.

We deal in people. Whether they're staff, elected officials, vendors, residents, or stakeholders—we're constantly managing relationships and navigating the unpredictable world of human behavior. You can have all the technical knowledge in the world, but if you can't read someone's intentions, feel their sincerity (or lack of it), or know how much room to give them, you'll get blindsided—sooner or later.

Reading People

Reading people is more than just watching their facial expressions or listening to their tone of voice—it's about reading patterns. Do their words match their actions? Are they consistent in how they treat others? Do they act differently in a crowd than they do one on one?

Here is where watching people, listening to people—without talking or disrupting the flow of the situation—becomes important. Being able to read body language is critical, but even more so are facial expressions, and listening to vocabulary and lexicon, voice tone, and especially reading their eyes. People often reveal their true selves without realizing it.

Sometimes, reading people means picking up on what's *not* being said. Silence can be as telling as speech. In meetings, hallway interactions, and casual encounters—stay alert. Patterns reveal more than isolated moments. They reveal a level of interpersonal communication that gives you more insight into them.

Believing in People

Empathy plays a central role in leadership. Believing in people allows us to build teams, nurture talent, and lead with compassion. More often than not, people just need one person to believe in them for them to rise.

But belief must come with accountability. Don't confuse belief with blindness. Believing in someone doesn't mean ignoring the signs when they go off track. It's about supporting them while also keeping expectations and standards clear.

Getting to know your colleagues is important. Know their families, their children's names, their pets. These personal details build trust and make you relatable. When things go wrong—and they will—it places you in a position where they seek you out, not the other way around. Spend time each week walking the departments, checking in with staff, and being visible in the community. These relationships matter.

Trusting People

Trust is sacred—and dangerous. Give it slowly. Test it continually. And when it's broken, address it directly.

But when you find someone you trust with your reputation, your peace of mind, and your career—keep them close. Whether it's a deputy, a longtime assistant, or even a council member you've weathered storms with, empower them. Give them the authority to guide you, push back, or slow you down when needed. These people help you think more clearly and prevent you from isolating yourself.

Trust is not a gift. It's a process.

And never blindly trust what you are told or what you hear. Know your audience and understand their motives.

Especially when it comes from an elected official. I have had some wonderful, elected officials over the years, and they are genuine, but until you know where they stand, just be cautious.

They may say "trust me," "do me a favor," or "don't worry about that—it's not important." These are red flags. Sometimes they mean well. But at the end of the day, they are elected. They don't work for you—you work for them. And their priorities, relationships, and insecurities shift quickly.

They may want your blind trust. But you don't need to give it.

Just don't let them know that.

You can smile, nod, and move forward cautiously—but never abandon your professional compass.

Jealousy among elected officials is common. It's not petty—it's political. The perception of closeness you share with one elected will shape how others view and treat you. They'll question your loyalty, your neutrality, and your intent.

One council member might see you laughing with another and think you're playing favorites. Or worse, they may believe you're conspiring. This can cost you trust, support, and eventually—your job.

You must walk the tightrope of being accessible without being owned, respectful without being a pushover, and involved without becoming indebted.

Trust in this field is earned through consistency, discretion, and humility. Give it with care, and guard it with vigilance.

How You Communicate Matters

Communication is everything. What you say, how you say it, when you say it—it all matters. Especially in public service.

In a large city, you might fade into the noise. But in small or mid-sized communities, your words carry weight. A short email can travel fast. A misunderstood comment in a public meeting can spark headlines. So how do you protect yourself?

If someone sends you a two-page email, respond with: "Come see me to discuss". Just respond tactfully, you don't want to start adversarial.

Not only is it more personal, but it also protects context, tone, and intention. Emotional nuances don't translate well in writing. And more importantly—it could be a trap.

Emails are public records. The public can request them pursuant to statutes in your state. Your tone, your brevity, your leadership style are on display. Why risk being misinterpreted or politically targeted because of an email? So, keep it short and to the point – leave out any commentary or emotion.

This extends to text messages and phone calls. You never know who's recording or listening. In some states, only one party has to consent to being recorded. Don't give anyone that kind of control over your voice. That's power you never get back.

But communication isn't just about crisis avoidance—it's about connection.

Sometimes, walking through a park and saying hello to the maintenance workers matters more than any policy memo or staff meeting.

They want to see you. They want to feel seen. They want to talk to you and feel that what they do matters.

And truthfully—it does.

I remember once walking through a city park, and one of the grass maintenance technicians stopped me. He said,

"Hey, I'm not sure what's happening, but if we had access to more rakes and shovels, I could probably do a better job. But they always lock them up and we can't get to them, so it's hard to do things the right way."

That small conversation stayed with me.

It reminded me that listening to everyone—regardless of title or their job—is a leadership duty. That one moment changed how I thought about access, tools, and the simple fixes that make people feel empowered.

What that technician needed wasn't just a rake—he needed to be heard. That also means, these interactions will never happen if you are not approachable.

Make time to communicate in person. Make time to check in. That kind of leadership doesn't go unnoticed—and it builds more loyalty than any bonus or recognition program ever could.

Caution Without Paranoia

This job can easily turn you paranoid. You deal with backdoor deals, shifting alliances, and sometimes outright sabotage. But don't let that eat away at your leadership soul.

Approach each situation with caution—but not fear. Optimism—but not naïveté.

Also—take care of yourself. If you research to see how many municipalities or counties over 20,000 population have a City Manager or Administrator, you will find that fewer than 10,000 people in the U.S. hold this job at any level of municipal government. It's elite, exhausting, and endlessly demanding.

Find time to relax. Do something fun. Exercise. Eat well. Travel. Laugh. Be human.

I spent the first twenty years of my career working 100+ hours a week, always on call. It's not sustainable. It wears you down mentally, emotionally, and physically. It dulls your thinking and kills your creativity.

Know when to rest. Know when to walk away from a moment, a meeting, or even a week. You can't lead if you're burned out.

Follow Up, Follow Through

One of the greatest habits you can develop is to follow through with intentionality. Don't assume someone will remember. Don't assume you will either.

Write personal notes every day. These aren't for your team. They're for you. But take them home—never leave them in your office. These are your private thoughts and reflections. In the wrong hands, they could be misunderstood or weaponized.

Also—surround yourself with one or two people who truly have your back. Maybe it's your deputy, or your assistant. Maybe it's a director you've built trust with. Give them the space to question you. Let them pull you aside and say, "Slow down." Let them help you stay on track and see what you don't.

The Power of Asking (or Not Asking) the Right Questions

"Never ask a question you don't already know the answer to. And never ask the question you don't want the answer to."

These are two entirely different things, though people often confuse them.

"Don't ask what you don't already know" is strategic. You're testing knowledge. You want to see if someone will admit, lie, or mislead you without prompting. Let them answer without guidance—this exposes truth, ego, and authenticity.

"Don't ask what you don't want to know" is a legal rule. In government, what you know becomes what you're responsible for. If you uncover something unethical or illegal, you may be legally required to act—even if you weren't prepared to. So don't ask unless you're ready for the consequences of knowing.

Know the difference. Both principles can save your career.

Final Thoughts

At the heart of this chapter is a single, powerful truth:

As a manager and leader, your greatest responsibility is awareness of people, your surroundings, and the issues that shape your organization.

This awareness isn't passive. It's active, ongoing, and should occupy a large portion of your professional energy every single day. You're not just managing policies or budgets, you're managing people, and people are dynamic, emotional, and complex.

You need to know what's happening in your departments, what's being said in the halls, and where tension might be brewing before it boils over. That means being present, being available, and being alert.

But awareness also means perspective.

Whether you're the city manager or a maintenance technician, we're all part of the same organization. We may have different jobs, but we share the same mission—to serve our community with integrity, efficiency, and pride.

Treat everyone with the respect you expect in return.

Titles come and go. Positions change. But character—how you treat others—is what people remember, and it's what builds a culture of mutual respect.

Lead by example. Show up for people. Watch carefully. Listen deeply. And never forget that in the end, you're just one part of a bigger purpose.

◆ Chapter 4 Summary

Read everyone. Believe selectively. Trust slowly. But when you do trust—do so fully. Remember trust, but verify.

Chapter 5: The Endgame

There's a moment in every public servant's career when they start to hear the clock ticking a little louder. It doesn't matter if you're five years out or five months out from retirement, once the end feels real, your thoughts shift.

You begin to ask questions like:

- Should I just hold on and play it safe?

- Can I afford to take this risk right now?

- What happens if I push too hard and lose it all?

- Am I finishing strong… or just trying to finish?

This chapter is about those moments. About the decisions that come when your career is closer to the end than the beginning. When your pension feels more important than your progress. And when you must choose whether to finish for yourself—or finish for the community you serve.

The Pension Paradox

There is no shame in wanting to secure your future. You've likely given two or three decades of service to cities or counties, often with stress that isn't visible from the outside. Political battles, late-night emergencies, budget shortfalls, lawsuits, hostile councils—this job comes with a cost.

So when managers begin to edge toward retirement, it's understandable to start playing it safer. The closer you get to the end, the more the fear creep in. The fear of losing what you've worked your entire life for. The fear of one misstep undoing decades of service. And that fear doesn't just weigh on your decisions – it weighs on you confidence.

Why? Because there's a pension on the line. And that pension isn't just about money, it represents everything you've worked for. And losing it because of a political misstep or sudden dismissal would be devastating.

But here's where the real question lies:

Are you willing to trade impact for security?

It's not easy to say yes or no. Because many times, the risks are real.

But if you're not careful, you stop leading and start coasting. You become a placeholder instead of a change-maker. The problems don't get solved; they just get passed on to the next person.

And whether you admit it or not, you feel it. You know when you're hesitating. You know when you're shrinking back. You know when you're no longer the leader you used to be. People know when you're collecting a check and bidding your time. They can feel the difference between someone going through the motions and someone still driving with purpose.

You're doing no one any good—especially not yourself—by hiding behind a desk and waiting out the clock. In fact, I've told every elected official I've worked for the same thing:

> Leadership has never been a desk job. The moment you stop showing up in the organization, you stop leading it.

Because this job isn't about managing from a swivel chair.

It's about being out in the community. Walking the halls. Talking to public works crews. Sitting in on planning sessions. Visiting the library, the parks, the police and fire stations, and every corner of your city or county. It's about showing up, not just signing off.

Any governing body can hire someone to sit at a desk and delegate. They can hire any clown to point fingers, push paper, and say, "You do this," or "You do that."

But it takes a leader to lead—not drive a desk.

The Final Years Matter Most

The truth is, the last few years of your service can be the most influential of your career. You've seen the battles. You know the personalities. You've gained political resilience and the ability to navigate complexity.

Those last few years are when you should be bolder. Because you know how. Because you've earned it.

The people around you—especially your staff—can feel the difference between someone who is holding on and someone who is still pushing forward.

If you coast, they feel it.

If you lean in, they respond to it.

And that ripple effect is what creates lasting change in a city—not policies, but people inspired by purpose.

The Emotional Toll and the Mental Shift

Let's be honest. Getting to the end isn't just a physical or financial milestone—it's an emotional and psychological journey.

There are days when you're just tired. When it feels like the politics never stop, the criticism never ends, and you're asked to justify every breath you take. And in those moments, it's tempting to say, "I'll just keep my head down. I've earned the right to glide."

But that's where this job will test your soul.

Because if you give in to early, you rob yourself of the chance to see what you're truly capable of in the hardest stretch of your career.   If you are there just to "Keep the Lights On", you should look at turning them off and look at moving on.

You'll leave the job with a pension, yes. But also, with lingering regret that you could have done more, spoken up, or taken a final stand on something that mattered.

Finishing Strong: What It Really Means

To finish strong means you make a choice, it doesn't mean burning bridges or charging into every battle. It means choosing wisely. Speaking deliberately. Leading with clarity. And knowing when to take a stand because your legacy is worth it.

It also means mentoring those around you—preparing the next generation of leaders. If you're not building successors or investing in your team's growth, you're not finishing well—you're just finishing.

Some of the most powerful leadership you can demonstrate is teaching, not doing. Guiding, not commanding. And showing others how to manage storms with grace and wisdom.

A Warning from the Field

Your silence protects no one – least of all you. Staying quiet for comfort is not the same as maintaining professionalism. Also, at the same time you are shortchanging those that look toward you for mentorship and guidance. You should continue your path for them.

There's no such thing as "coasting safely." You're either navigating… or drifting. And drifting leads to shipwrecks.

Ask Yourself Daily

- Am I leading or surviving?

- Is this decision for me—or for the community?

- Am I preparing the organization for my exit—or just preparing my exit?

These aren't comfortable questions. But they're necessary.

Because how you finish says more about your character than how you began.

Final Thoughts

In this profession, legacy matters. Not the plaques or the thank-you speeches—but the quiet moments when your team remembers how you stood firm, or how you lifted them up, or how you put the city above your career.

You can retire with a pension and still feel like you left something unfinished.

Or you can retire knowing that in your final days, you did your most meaningful work, you finished strong, stronger than when you started.

You are the steward of your ending. Make it count.

◆ Chapter 5 Summary

The final chapter of your career should be written with courage, not caution.

Chapter 6: Why Even Have a Box

Early in my career, I was told something that sounded wise at the time: *"Think outside the box!"* Years later, when people encouraged me to *"make your box bigger,"* I tried that too. But after three decades in public service, working through politics, management challenges, and organizational transformation, I came to a realization far more important than either piece of advice:

Why have a box at all?

Because the moment you accept that you operate inside a box—no matter how large—you have already accepted boundaries that limit creativity, restrict innovation, narrow participation, and stunt both personal and organizational growth.

The Myth of the Box

The box is not just a metaphor. It becomes a mindset that defines the limits of what people believe they are allowed to do. It influences how staff perceive their work, how they approach problems, and how they evaluate opportunities.

Here's what most leaders never say out loud:

When you create a box, you control how people think.

The box tells people:

- Stay here.

- Think this way.

- Don't cross these boundaries.

- Don't experiment unless someone approves it.

- Don't create anything that challenges the structure.

When a leader defines "the box," they also define:

- Which ideas are acceptable

- Which risks are permissible

- How creativity is interpreted

- Whose voices count

- And how far an employee feels empowered to go

The box seems harmless at first—orderly, predictable, manageable. But over time, it becomes a quiet barrier to growth.

When the Box Becomes a Barrier

Boxes feel safe because they create familiar patterns. But familiarity kills innovation.

When staff are boxed in, two predictable symptoms emerge:

1. They stop thinking for themselves.

Employees learn the edges of the box and simply stop pushing outward.

2. They become dependent on you.

They wait for direction. They fear breaking rules. They ask permission instead of taking initiative.

You didn't hire people to operate inside boundaries. You hired them to think, build, solve, innovate, collaborate, and serve the community.

But the box suffocates that instinct.

And the more structured and confining the box becomes, the more silent the workforce gets.

The Hidden Danger: You Become the Box

Here's the uncomfortable truth:

If you're not careful, YOU become the box.

You become the boundary. You define what is possible. And you unintentionally train your staff to limit their thinking to what *you* would do.

Every time you say:

- "We don't do that here."

- "Stick to the process."

- "This is how we've always handled it."

- "Let's not reinvent the wheel."

…you shrink the space your people feel safe to think in.

You begin controlling not just decisions—but their daily thought process.

That's not leadership. That's containment.

Managers Who Use the Box Are Not Leaders

This is where most people never go, but it needs to be said plainly:

Managers who rely on the box to control their colleagues are not leaders.

They may have the title. They may have authority. But the behavior is not leadership—it's fear disguised as structure.

A leader removes walls. A controller builds them. Leaders expand people. Controllers restrict them. Leaders want others to rise. Controllers want people to stay manageable.

When a manager uses the "box theory" to direct, limit, or constrain others, it becomes a control mechanism—a way to manage thinking rather than inspire it.

Control produces compliance. Leadership produces excellence.

Leadership Without Walls

Leadership without walls is not chaotic. It is purposeful freedom.

It means:

- Encouraging ideas that challenge the status quo
- Helping employees find answers you never would have considered
- Giving people permission to take risks
- Allowing room for safe failure
- Letting staff build solutions, not wait for approval

A leader's responsibility is to create a space where people feel safe enough to think, brave enough to try, and supported enough to push beyond what they thought possible.

When you remove the box, people step into their potential.

And when people step into their potential, the organization transforms.

Creating a No-Box Culture

A no-box culture is not the absence of structure—it is the presence of possibility.

To build it:

- Replace rigid rules with clear principles

- Explain the "why" and allow staff to determine the "how"

- Reward innovative thinking

- Encourage cross-departmental collaboration

- Celebrate ideas, not just outcomes

- Remove habitual boundaries

- Invite staff to challenge assumptions

Ask your people: "If there were no box at all, how would you approach this?"

Their answer will reveal two things:

1. Their true creative potential.

2. The chains you didn't realize you placed on them.

◆ **Chapter 6 Summary — Why Even Have a Box?**

The "box" doesn't expand potential—it limits it. It restricts growth, controls how employees think, and quietly shapes what people believe they are allowed to contribute.

Managers who use the box as a boundary for their colleagues aren't leading—they're controlling. True leadership removes those boundaries entirely and empowers people to innovate, collaborate, and grow without constraints.

Leadership thrives when the box disappears.

Chapter 7: Opportunity to Excel (OTE)

About fifteen years ago, I recognized a pattern in every city organization I worked with: talented employees plateaued not because they lacked ability—but because they lacked opportunity.

That's when I created a simple but powerful philosophy called OTE: Opportunity to Excel.

It wasn't a program. It wasn't a policy. It wasn't a scheduled workshop.

It was a mindset shift—one that challenged every department to intentionally create opportunities for their people to grow, shine, and lead.

What OTE Really Means

OTE is not about promotions. It's not about raises. It's not about climbing a ladder someone else built.

It's about:

- Unlocking potential

- Expanding capability

- Encouraging exploration

- Building confidence

- And helping employees see what they could become

The core question of OTE is simple:

"What are you doing to give your people opportunities to excel?"

This one question reshapes how managers think about development.

The OTE Framework

Each department implementing OTE uses four core steps:

1. Identify Strengths and Barriers

Look at:

- What staff do well

- What stands in their way

- Where potential is being wasted

- How workflow or culture restricts creativity

2. Build Growth Pathways

Not generic training—intentional development:

- Role rotations

- Cross-department exposure

- Mentorship from subject-matter experts

- Stretch assignments

- Responsibility-based growth

3. Promote Ownership

Give people space to lead:

- Projects

- Pilots

- Improvements

- Events

- Initiatives

Ownership builds internal leaders. Internal leaders build organizational strength.

4. Celebrate Progress

Recognition is a multiplier. Celebrate:

- Effort

- Initiative

- Improvement

- Collaboration

- Innovation

People who feel seen will always do more.

The Ripple Effect of OTE

When people are given opportunities to excel:

- They become more creative

- They take initiative

- They collaborate more

- They stay longer

- They care more deeply

- They trust leadership more readily

More importantly, OTE teaches people how to see opportunities in each other.

When a workforce develops the habit of recognizing potential, the organization shifts from maintenance mode to growth mode.

OTE and Organizational Resilience

Here's what most leaders underestimate:

OTE strengthens your organization's ability to survive external pressures.

When your staff is engaged, growing, and empowered, the organization becomes more resilient during:

- Budget cuts

- Political turnover

- Shifting priorities

- Leadership changes

- Public criticism

- Council pressure

- Emergencies and crises

A culture built on opportunity is a culture that can weather the storm.

When people believe in themselves, they don't fold under pressure— they step forward.

Leaders as Enablers

A leader's role in OTE is simple:

- Remove barriers

- Provide direction

- Offer guidance

- Encourage courage

- And most importantly… Pass on the ability to see potential in others

This is how leadership multiplies. When people are taught how to identify potential in others, the entire organization becomes a leadership engine.

◆ Chapter 7 Summary — Opportunity to Excel (OTE)

OTE is more than a program—it's a leadership philosophy. It challenges managers to intentionally create opportunities for people to rise, grow, and lead.

When people are empowered, organizations become more resilient and capable of surviving budget pressures, political shifts, management changes, and crises.

If you want your organization, your team, and your community to grow, you must create opportunities for everyone to excel.

Chapter 8: Talking, Listening, Hearing

In a world driven by noise, the greatest power you have as a municipal executive is to know when to speak, when to listen, and when to actually hear what's not being said. That sounds simple, but it's one of the hardest skills to master in leadership. Most people assume those three words mean the same thing. They don't. And in your role, confusing them can cost you trust, authority, and even your job.

Of all three, the most important is hearing. Talking may make you visible, and listening may make you approachable—but hearing is what makes you credible. Hearing requires a full presence of mind, not just attention to words, but to tone, to intent, to body language, and to context. It means grasping what's truly at stake beyond the surface. Without that, you're not leading—you're just reacting.

Talking Isn't Leading

Let's start with the simplest mistake: the belief that talking equates to leading. We've all met the elected official, department head, or even colleague who thinks their volume or verbosity equals value. It doesn't. Speaking should be intentional. If you're constantly talking, explaining, justifying, commanding—you're not allowing space for your team or your community to show you where they are.

As a manager, your words carry weight. That means when you speak, it should be on purpose, with purpose, and for a purpose. Every time you open your mouth in a council meeting, public forum, staff huddle, or hallway conversation, you're making an impression. You are being recorded by memory, by public record, and sometimes by phone. Speak clearly. Speak with empathy. Speak with intention.

But also know when not to speak at all.

Listening Isn't Just Being Quiet

Listening is active. Listening is a skill. It's not simply sitting still while someone else talks. It's asking yourself:

- What are they really trying to say?

- What's the tone behind their words?

- What are they not saying that I should be picking up on?

As a city or county manager, you'll constantly be approached by people with agendas—sometimes clear, sometimes hidden. If you listen only to respond, you'll miss the point. If you listen just to react, you're already off balance. But if you listen to understand, you'll learn more than any formal report could ever tell you.

People also need to see that you're listening. Don't seem distracted. Don't look at your phone or your watch. Watch your own body language, your posture, and especially your eyes. Are you looking through them or at them? Are you nodding in genuine recognition, or just trying to signal that you want them to finish?

Most of the time, people just want someone to listen. Not to fix things, not to argue, not to take sides—but just to let them speak. When you give someone the space to talk, you'll find they often start to work through the issue themselves. They'll hear their own logic out loud. They'll slow down their thinking, clarify their message, and even correct themselves in real time. Don't interrupt them. Let them finish. Then—when they're done—repeat back what you believe they're asking, or what you understood them to mean. This gives them clarity, shows you care, and makes sure both of you are actually talking about the same thing. That reflection is one of the most powerful tools in any manager's toolkit. It builds understanding and prevents miscommunication before it starts.

Hearing Is Where Leadership Begins

Hearing in leadership is like playing chess. Most people focus on the move that was just made—they react to the surface play. But effective leaders study the board, consider what the move represents, and anticipate the motivation behind it. Every piece moved has intent. Every pause has weight. Hearing is about seeing the game beyond the board.

In government, every conversation carries strategy. You don't just listen to a staff member complaining about a policy, you hear what that policy is doing to morale. You don't just listen to an elected official pushing for a project—you hear the political pressure they're under, the alliances they're protecting, or the commitments they've made. And you don't just listen to the community yelling at a meeting—you hear the fear, confusion, or distrust that's driving their frustration.

To hear is to translate emotion into insight—to recognize patterns, motives, and consequences before they unfold. That's where trust is built. That's where leadership grows.

And just as important as what you hear is how you show you're hearing.

The number one thing you don't do when you're truly hearing someone is take notes. It might seem practical, but it often feels cold, calculated, or even threatening. It can give the impression that:

- You aren't really paying attention.
- You're not capable of remembering on your own.
- Or worse, that you're documenting ammunition for later use.

None of those impressions build trust.

If something must be recorded, wait until after the conversation ends. Step aside, return to your office, and document what's needed privately. In the moment, your presence, focus, and ability to recall what was said will carry more power than any notebook ever could.

Train your mind to listen with retention. Practice summarizing back the essence of what someone has said—not only for clarity, but for memory. When people realize you heard them, remembered them, and acted on their words, you earn more than their respect. You earn their confidence. And that's how leadership moves from reaction to strategy—one conversation at a time.

But the board doesn't only teach you about others—it teaches you about yourself. True hearing forces you to listen inwardly. You start to recognize the moves you make out of habit, fear, pride, or frustration. You hear your own defensiveness before it speaks, your impatience before it shows, your bias before it blinds you. Self-awareness becomes part of the same game. When you hear yourself with honesty, you sharpen judgment, improve timing, and lead with humility. Because the only way to hear others with clarity is to quiet the noise within.

Practice Listening with Intention

Spend a few minutes each day in silence—not just physical silence, but conversational silence. Visit a department. Walk the halls. Ask a question and let the pause breathe. Don't fill every moment with your voice.

You'd be amazed by what people will tell you when you just let them talk.

And that includes the people who rarely get asked.

People want to be heard. You need to make that happen.

Caution: Emails, Texts, and Traps

Now let's talk about the dangerous side of talking—email, texting, and over-explaining.

Unfortunately, people have taken to the ease of email and the proverbial CYA, to communicate more often. However, it is not inherently productive when managing an ever-changing environment that is personal, political, and open for complete public scrutiny. Don't over communicate with email, convenient yes – bad for so many other reasons.

Why? Because tone, emotion, concern, and intent are nearly impossible to convey in writing—and public records laws mean those emails could be published or FOIA (Federal Information Act) at any moment. Don't let someone trap you into looking cold, dismissive, or incompetent by parsing your tone.

Remember that your response via text or email does not contain any of your facial expressions, body language, tone, concern, or emotion—and you never want to attempt to convey those in a written message. Misinterpretation is inevitable, and even a well-intended message can be twisted to suggest you don't care or that you're being unprofessional. In sensitive roles like yours, perception matters as much as reality.

That same caution applies to texts and phone calls too. You never know who's recording. You don't know who's screen shotting. You don't know who's building a case against you while pretending to ask a question. And even the most innocent voicemail can come back to haunt you if replayed out of context.

The same goes for talking on the phone—it's just too easy to record these days. Just be aware and be knowledgeable. Know when to engage and when to step back. If something feels off or overly formal, it's probably because you're being baited. You don't have to be paranoid—but you do have to be careful.

Being the manager means everyone is watching—your team, your critics, the public, and especially the media. Whether good or bad, people are observing how you communicate. Don't help them attack you with your own messages. One wrong sentence taken out of context can be turned into a headline, a campaign issue, or a reason to question your leadership.

Be strategic. Be simple. Be present. Whenever possible, speak face to face—where your intent is clear, your message is direct, and your leadership is evident.

Getting to Know Your People

If you want to lead, listen. But if you want to lead well, connect.

Know your department heads' spouses' names. Know the name of their kids. Ask about their dog. If someone's mom just went into the hospital, follow up on it. That's not small talk—that's building human capital. Those personal touches matter more than a title or directive ever will. These are just suggestions, but you need to find your own way to interact and personalize your relationships.

Spend as much time out of the office as you reasonably can, getting to know your staff at every level. Recognize that in some organizations, especially large ones, you may never know every single employee—but that doesn't mean they shouldn't know you. Make yourself visible. Be accessible. Walk the halls, visit the shops, eat in the breakroom, ride in the city truck. When people see you as more than just a nameplate on a door, trust begins to form.

Getting to know your people isn't just a gesture, it's a strategy. When difficult conversations arise, or a complaint lands on your desk, or you're called to make a tough decision involving staff, the relationships you've built can help you read between the lines. You may already know what's motivating someone before they say it out loud. That's an advantage—just let them finish.

Because knowing your people helps you predict behavior, defuse issues before they escalate, and lead with empathy. It refines your management style and strengthens your engagement with the team, the organization, and ultimately, the community you serve.

There's no shortcut for this. It takes time. But it's time well spent.

Final Thought: Listening Is Leadership

This chapter is not about staying silent—it's about becoming intentional. Leadership isn't found in volume, reaction, or fast answers. It's found in pause, in observation, and in the strength to wait and understand before you speak.

The best leaders aren't the ones who always have something to say, they're the ones others seek out because they know their words will be measured, meaningful, and grounded in understanding.

In your role, every email, every text, every phone call, and every word carries weight. But it's not just what you say—it's when, how, and why you say it. Whether you're addressing a city council, engaging with a community member, or walking through a public works yard, you are the tone-setter. Your ability to hear what's truly being said, recognize what isn't, and respond with both empathy and awareness is what separates managers from leaders.

And remember this: everyone is watching your staff, your elected officials, the community. They're watching how you listen, how you react, how you engage, and how you show up. Don't give them ammunition to question your integrity. Give them reason to believe in your leadership.

Be present. Be strategic. Be real. Because leadership isn't loud. It's steady, it's consistent, and it starts with hearing.

◆ Chapter 8 Summary

True leadership begins with intentional listening and hearing beyond words. Every action, message, and silence leaves a trail—so choose each with awareness. Be the leader they remember for your presence, not just your position.

Chapter 9: Leading for Legacy or Last Paycheck?

This chapter goes into more detail about your final years as it is of significant importance and sets a tone for you and staff and community based upon facing potential complacency.

The Pension Paradox in Public Service

At some point in your public service career, especially in those final years, you're faced with a quiet but pressing question: *Am I finishing this race for me, or for the community I serve?* The question might not be spoken aloud, but it echoes in your decisions, in your motivation, and in how others perceive your leadership.

Let's be honest—many managers reach the last five to ten years of their careers and begin to drift. The finish line is in sight, and with it comes the temptation to coast. To show up but not step up. To collect a paycheck and pad the pension without rocking any boats. After all, why take risks now? You've paid your dues. You've earned your time.

But here's the truth: *Everyone sees it.* Your staff, your elected officials, your community, they all know when you've shifted into neutral. And when they do, your credibility slowly starts to erode.

The Driving Question: Are You Leading or Simply Lasting?

There's a difference between leadership and occupancy. A leader pushes the organization forward with energy, with vision, and with purpose. An occupant simply holds the seat.

I've told every elected body I've ever worked for: *"If you see me behind my desk 90% of the time, I'm not doing my job."* Any one of them can hire a warm body to sit in that chair and sign off on paperwork. But it takes a manager, a leader, to be present—in departments, in neighborhoods, at public events, and inside the organization. If I'm not seen, I'm not leading.

Leadership in your final years should not be about self-preservation. It should be about legacy. What do you want to leave behind? What condition will the city or county be in when your keys hit the desk on your final day? Who have you mentored? What projects have you built that will outlast your contract?

Because this isn't just a job. It's a community. And when your paycheck becomes your only priority, your community pays the price.

The Pension Paradox: Safety or Service?

The pension system—while necessary and earned—is a double-edged sword. It creates stability, but it can also create stagnation. Many managers begin protecting themselves – not because they've grown lazy, but because the spark that once made them bold now flickers under the weight of political risk. A controversial decision, a political blow-up, a misstep in a high-profile moment—any one of these can cost them their job and their pension security. So, they shrink back.

But the real risk is not doing the job poorly, it's doing it halfway.

When fear drives your decisions, you're no longer managing. You're surviving. And survival isn't the same as leadership. Leadership requires movement, change, accountability, and risk. No one wants a manager who's just counting days. They want someone who shows up like it's still their first year on the job.

The Cost of Playing It Safe

Let's be clear: playing it safe doesn't mean avoiding conflict, it means avoiding responsibility. You stop challenging bad ideas. You start rubber-stamping agendas. You nod along instead of pushing back. You protect your title instead of your team.

And the worst part? Your team starts to notice. They start to model your apathy. Department heads begin showing up for the paycheck too. Initiative dries up. Innovation flatlines. Momentum stalls.

The problem with playing it safe is that it doesn't stay invisible for long. Staff begin to match your energy. Department heads adjust to your lowered expectations. Even the community notices when the city manager's presence starts to fade. Disengagement, no matter how carefully concealed, always leaks out in tone, posture, urgency, and presence.

The organization mirrors the energy of its leadership.

But it doesn't stop at the organization—this disengagement reverberates into the community. Your presence, or lack thereof, becomes obvious. Whatever your internal motivations are—fear, burnout, self-preservation, you might think you're hiding it well. But you're not. Disguising disengagement over a long period is almost impossible. People can feel it, even if they can't name it.

Not only will your staff and colleagues notice, but the community will also feel it too. And the deeper you bury your motivation, the more visible it becomes. Eventually, it will show in your tone, your body language, your availability, and even your posture in meetings. People may not articulate what changed, but they can sense when leadership has lost its edge. And once they sense it, they begin rewriting your story long before you've written the final chapter. Potentially worst of all, they begin to undermine you behind your back, and look for ways to push you out faster.

And when they do? That's when the clock starts ticking.

If people notice your lack of presence or purpose, they will quietly start to question your leadership. Elected officials, staff, and even residents may begin forming their own narratives. Over time, those narratives evolve into conversations. And before you realize it, you're being written out of your own organization's story. They'll stop confiding in you, they'll start circling around you, and soon, they'll begin crafting an early exit plan—one that you're not invited to shape.

So, what do you do about it?

This is where you must take responsibility—not just for others, but for your own energy. I've found that the best way to counteract this slide is to re-engage deliberately. Find new areas of interest. Get involved in mentoring your staff or developing future leaders. Volunteer to help with a regional project. Join a strategic planning effort that excites you. Don't do it for appearances—do it because you need it. Your continued engagement will show through, and people will take notice. They'll feel your investment not only in the job but in *them*.

This is also a good time to start quietly educating and preparing a few trusted individuals for what might come next—whether you're six months or six years away from leaving. Succession planning isn't about exciting, it's about legacy. It's about caring for the organization beyond your own tenure.

Don't ever be afraid that you're training someone to take your job. That's not weakness—that's leadership. Weak leaders hoard knowledge out of insecurity. Strong leaders build others up so the mission continues without disruption. Preparing for a smooth transition shows that you care about the people, the culture, and the future of the organization—not just your office or your paycheck.

When your team sees that you're still thinking ahead, still building, still pouring into the organization, they'll respond with renewed purpose. You set the tone. Always have. Always will.

Reclaiming Purpose in Your Final Years

For many managers, those final years in public service feel like a balancing act between winding down and holding on. You're experienced. You're seasoned. You've weathered political storms, budget crises, staffing turnovers, and public blowback. But now, you might feel the creeping fatigue—the slow erosion of passion, the loss of urgency, the dulling of purpose.

That's normal. But it's not inevitable. Your experience becomes an asset only if you continue to apply it. If not, it becomes a silent archive that no one benefits from.

This phase of your career is not just about survival—it's about legacy. And it's about asking yourself the hard question: "Am I still here to lead, or am I just staying because it's comfortable?"

If you're just hanging on until retirement, it will show. If you're avoiding change or silencing your voice because you don't want to risk upsetting the balance, it will show. And once that begins, your impact starts to shrink, even before your exit.

But here's the opportunity: these years can be your most powerful. You now possess institutional memory, deep relationships, strategic insight, and a resilience that only comes from experience. Use them. Mentor a future leader. Revisit a community initiative you never had time for. Walk the halls and remind your team of their value. Listen more. Speak intentionally. Set the tone.

This is where legacy is built.

Someone once told me that I may never be a millionaire or have my name on a building named after me. And that struck me. It was honest—and freeing. Because in the very same breath, they added something that stayed with me forever: "But you see that community center over there? You helped plan and make that happen. You see that aquatic center? You fought for it. That new police station downtown? Your leadership got it built. And every one of those buildings has a small plaque in the corner—with your name on it."

That. Is. Legacy.

You don't need your name on street signs or billboards. You need to know that the work you did mattered—that it still stands, still serves, and still reflects the values you carried into every decision. That plaque isn't about recognition, it's about proof. Proof that in a position where outcomes take years and progress is often quiet; you made a mark.

Reclaiming purpose in your final years is not about chasing titles or trying to fix everything you couldn't before. It's about reminding yourself why you began. And if you've done this job right, you'll realize that your legacy isn't in your job title—it's in the lives you changed, the buildings you helped raise, and the community you helped shape.

Final Thought: What Will They Say When You're Gone?

At the end of your career, when you walk out of that city hall or county administration building for the last time, what will people say?

Not what they post online. Not what's written in your formal evaluation. Not even what's said during your retirement ceremony. But what will your staff whisper to one another when your name comes up? What will your elected officials recall in private moments? What will community members feel when they walk by a project you helped make possible?

Will they remember you as the person who led with courage, clarity, and compassion? Or will they remember the version of you that played it safe, kept your head down, and stopped fighting for progress when the finish line came into view?

The final years of your career aren't about coasting—they're about finishing with purpose. Because whether you know it or not, people are always watching. Your staff, the public, and even your critics can feel when you've started to check out. They can sense the difference between a leader still driving toward a vision and one who's just riding out the clock.

And if they see you pulling back, they'll respond in kind. They may begin to challenge your leadership, question your relevance, or even try to write your ending for you.

But it doesn't have to be this way.

You can reinvest. You can mentor. You can engage with your community in ways you haven't before. You can plan for succession—not as a sign of stepping away, but as a sign of your strength. Weak leaders fear being replaced. Strong leaders ensure their organization is ready when they go.

And through it all, you can model what it means to leave the job the right way—with dignity, with presence, and with continued commitment to the people you serve.

Your legacy isn't measured in the length of your tenure or the title on your door. It's measured in the impact you leave behind, the trust you built, the staff you grew, and the community you strengthened.

So, ask yourself now—not when you're packing up your office: What will they say when I'm gone?

Then lead in a way that answers the question... without you ever having to say a word.

◆ Chapter 9 Summary

The true endgame of leadership isn't about how long you last—it's about how purposefully you finish. Legacy is built in your final steps, not your first. Lead with presence, mentor with intention, and plan for what's next. What they say after you're gone depends entirely on how you choose to leave.

Chapter 10: Let the Other Person Always Talk First

In this profession, silence is not just golden—it's strategic. One of the simplest, most powerful pieces of advice I give to emerging municipal executives is this: Let the other person talk first.

That principle may sound minor, even passive. But it is neither. It is rooted in deep emotional intelligence and tactical awareness. In high-stakes conversations—whether with staff, elected officials, community members, or consultants—what people say first often reveals what they value, what they fear, and what they want. When you give them the floor, you give yourself the upper hand.

You gain insight. You gain leverage. And, most importantly, you gain time to assess, respond, and lead with intentionality.

Of all the tools in your leadership toolbox, your actions, your words, and your presence are some of the most powerful. They set the tone before you say a word. Whether the person in front of you is an elected official, a resident, a business owner, a city employee, or even a member of the media—your role is to meet them where they are, not where you assume they should be.

Whether you're talking to a man or a woman, someone who is twenty or someone who is eighty, someone furious or someone fragile—you need to engage at their level, without talking down to them. That doesn't mean changing who you are. It means being present, attentive, and responsive in a way that builds trust.

Making Others Feel Safe to Speak

Making someone feel safe enough to talk to you is equally important. That safety doesn't come from your title, your office, or your credentials—it comes from your presence. It comes from showing that you are open, calm, and trustworthy. The setting matters just as much as your demeanor.

Don't hold difficult conversations in rooms filled with tension or distraction. Avoid sitting behind a desk like you're the judge and jury. Instead, create a space where people feel like they're being invited into a conversation—not summoned into an interrogation. Should you sit next to them, not across from them? Be mindful of posture, eye contact, and tone. When people feel emotionally and physically comfortable, they will open up. And when they open up, you learn more—faster, and with more honesty.

It's Not About Silence, It's About Control

Letting the other person talk first isn't about silence for silence's sake. It's about control—controlling the pace of the conversation, the emotional temperature, and the strategic landscape. When you talk first, you show your hand. When you wait, they show theirs.

I've been in hundreds of meetings where I sat down, nodded once, and said nothing for the first several minutes. You'd be amazed how quickly people fill the silence. They reveal concerns, perspectives, motivations—and sometimes secrets—they never planned on disclosing.

That's when the real work begins.

Elected Officials, Staff, and the Power of Listening

This strategy works with everyone: elected officials who are trying to sway you, staff members who are nervous to confront you, and even residents in a public meeting who come in angry and ready for a fight. Let them talk.

Let them vent. Let them explain. Let them get it out.

Sometimes, that's all they want.

Other times, you'll hear what they really need—and it won't be what they initially claimed. Your ability to sit quietly and listen will help you get to the root faster than any policy memo or report.

When you let people talk first, they will often feel more respected, more in control, and more willing to meet you halfway. That's a win for everyone.

Your Ego Doesn't Lead—Your Ears Do

A lot of managers feel the pressure to prove themselves in every conversation. They want to be the smartest person in the room; to show they're in charge, to deliver the perfect response before the question's even asked. But that mindset will sink you.

You don't prove you're a leader by dominating conversations. You prove it by knowing when not to.

True strength isn't in how quickly you speak—it's in how well you listen. If you don't feel the need to fill every silence, you're showing confidence. If you're comfortable letting others go first, you're showing control.

Leadership isn't about being the loudest. It's about being the clearest, the calmest, and the most thoughtful voice in the room—especially when that voice comes last.

Caution: Don't Use Silence to Manipulate

That said, silence is not a weapon. It's a tool. If you use it to make others feel small, confused, or uncertain, you've lost the point of leadership. Silence shouldn't be used to trap someone into saying something they regret or to exert power over someone in a vulnerable position.

The goal is clarity, not control.

Manipulative silence leads to broken trust, disengaged staff, and toxic environments. People will start to fear meetings with you, not welcome them. They'll shut down. They'll withhold. And eventually, they'll walk away—emotionally or literally.

So yes, let them talk first—but make it a safe, respectful invitation, not a silent test.

Case Example: The Consultant Who Overplayed

I once had a consultant from a neighboring city come into my office full of energy, sure he knew everything about a development proposal. He walked in with his laptop open, documents printed, and a pitch rehearsed. I let him talk.

And talk he did.

He spent nearly 25 minutes explaining every piece of the project—except the part that actually mattered to our community.

He had data. He had graphics. But he never once asked what we needed. He never once paused to get my input. And at the end of his performance, he leaned back and said, "What do you think?"

I simply replied, "You never asked me what I wanted."

The look on his face was priceless. It wasn't rude—it was honest. And it changed the tone of the rest of the meeting. That moment showed him that talking doesn't equal connecting. It showed him that presence requires more than PowerPoint.

Final Thought: The Best Leaders Say Less and Hear More

This chapter isn't about staying silent. It's about learning how to position yourself so that others feel seen, heard, and valued. When you lead with intentional silence—when you let others speak first, when you listen for meaning, and when you respond with clarity, you build relationships that last.

Your job isn't to be the smartest person in the room. It's to be the one others trust enough to speak to first.

Let them talk. Show them they matter. Then lead.

◆ Chapter 10 Summary

Letting others talk first isn't passive, it's powerful. Use silence to invite trust, not fear. Speak less, hear more, and let every conversation start with the voice that matters most—theirs.

Chapter 11: Enemies in the Hallway

In any leadership position, you will encounter friction. But in public service—particularly as a city or county manager—there's a unique strain of resistance that is quieter, more subversive, and far more dangerous: sabotage. It doesn't always look like open defiance or overt rejection. Often, it's subtle. A delay here. A miscommunication there. A smile with a knife behind the back.

These are the enemies in the hallway. And sometimes, they wear the same badge, sit in the same meetings, and smile during the same photo ops.

And sometimes, it may be the people you trust and the people you have confided in the most.

This is perhaps the hardest truth to face in leadership—that the ones you've mentored, promoted, or stood up for might be the same ones working behind the scenes to erode your credibility. It's painful. But it happens. Trust is a currency in leadership—and once spent, it doesn't always yield the return you expect. The very people who've shared quiet coffee conversations with you, who've been in your inner circle, who've called you "friend," may be working angles for themselves. Ego, ambition, or resentment—they all blur the lines.

Your job is to lead despite it.

Sabotage Doesn't Always Scream—Sometimes It Whispers

It's easy to spot someone who stands up at a public meeting and yells at you. That's theater. But the person who quietly leaks information to a reporter, who redirects a project behind your back, or who nods in agreement during a meeting only to undermine your decision afterward—that's the real threat.

This kind of sabotage is harder to detect because it operates within the system. It cloaks itself in professionalism. It thrives on ambiguity and plausible deniability. And it grows stronger the more you ignore it.

You must lead above all this. You cannot be phased. Yes—be concerned. Yes—be observant. But don't act on it directly in a way that reveals your hand. Keep your posture, stay calm, and remain strategic. Reacting impulsively to every whisper only feeds the saboteurs. Staying composed is your quiet power.

And remember what we discussed in the chapter on legacy: if you're mentally checking out—just sitting in the chair for a paycheck or a pension—you'll miss the subtle overtures or signals. You won't see the movements in the corners of the room, the small alliances forming, or the shifts in tone that hint at deeper motives.

That's why presence is everything. You must stay engaged. Even near the end of your career, even when burnout creeps in. Engagement is what keeps your awareness sharp, your intuition alert, and your leadership alive.

Recognizing sabotage requires heightened perception. Patterns matter. Sudden breakdowns in communication. Changes in behavior. Unexplained resistance. Staff who once collaborated now withholding. Those are your early signals. Listen to your intuition.

And always verify.

Ego Is a Management Wildcard

Ego is present in every organization. It walks the halls, sits at the boardroom table, and smiles in the staff photo. It's not always bad—confidence and ambition have their place. But when ego goes unchecked, it can become poison.

A department head who believes they should be in your chair. An elected official who wants to be the "real" power. A mid-level staffer who thinks they're the smartest person in the room. These egos will test your patience and your professionalism.

You cannot ignore ego, but you also cannot combat it with your own. Instead, you manage it. Feed it when appropriate, deflect it when necessary, and never let it dictate policy or decision-making.

Sometimes ego just wants to be heard or validated. Other times, it wants control. Learn which is which—and don't take either personally. Remember what may be personal to you is ego for them.

Hidden Agendas Don't Announce Themselves

Not everyone is going to tell you what they want—and that's exactly the point.

In municipal leadership, you'll encounter people whose goals aren't aligned with their words. A vendor says they're just offering help, but they're angling for a contract. A staff member claims to be asking questions, but they're really undermining a project. An elected official suggests an idea "just for discussion," but they've already promised it to a supporter.

This is where your ability to observe and interpret is vital. You need to learn how to hear what's not being said. Tone, timing, body language, who's in the room—these are all pieces of a larger puzzle.

But more importantly, this is where your follow-up and follow-through count the most.

If someone says they'll provide a report—follow up. If you commit to doing something—follow through. And if things change and you're unable to complete what you promised, don't let it disappear into the void. Return, report, and explain. Your credibility isn't just about what you deliver—it's about how you stay accountable when you can't deliver.

Doing so neutralizes hidden agendas before they can take root. It keeps you in control of the narrative. It ensures that people know you are paying attention—not just when something is easy or convenient, but especially when it's difficult or uncomfortable.

It also lets your team and the public know that transparency and accountability matter. That even if you're not perfect—and none of us are—you will always show up, close the loop, and own the process.

That, more than anything, builds a culture where hidden agendas can't thrive.

Professional Doesn't Mean Passive

Being professional doesn't mean being quiet. It doesn't mean taking abuse. And it certainly doesn't mean allowing yourself—or your staff—to be undermined publicly.

Too often, professionalism is mistaken for passivity. But in reality, being professional is about knowing when and how to stand your ground without becoming combative. It's the ability to maintain your presence and integrity in the face of conflict, misinformation, or manipulation.

That also means that when you're in the public domain, especially during a council or board meeting—you take full responsibility for your staff when something goes wrong. You don't deflect. You don't blame. You own the outcome and say, "We'll come back with a better solution." That's what a leader does.

Never throw your team under the bus. Even if they made a mistake, the moment you distance yourself from them publicly, you've broken the very trust and loyalty you rely on to function as a team. Your staff is also learning by example.

The same standard applies to positive recognition. If the board or public congratulates you for a successful project, don't absorb all the praise—pass it along. Recognize your director, your staff, the frontline employees who made it happen. That's not just good leadership—it's essential to team morale.

Taking all the credit is ego. Giving it away is leadership.

When you protect your team in hard moments and uplift them in the good ones, they'll stand by you. They'll go the extra mile. They'll stay engaged. Because they'll know you're not just in the back office, you're in their corner.

Build Quiet Alliances

Not every ally is loud. Some of your greatest supporters will be those who work behind the scenes—staff who step in when others try to undercut you, elected officials who vouch for your integrity in private conversations, or residents who write letters of support when critics get loud.

Cultivate these relationships. Not out of paranoia, but out of strategy. Every good leader needs trusted voices—people who see what you're facing and remind you why you're still standing.

These people are your grounding rods. Listen to them. Protect them. And never take them for granted.

Final Thought: Lead Like They're Watching—Because They Are

Leadership in the public sector is never a private act. Whether you realize it or not, every move you make—every meeting you attend, every conversation you have, every reaction you give—is on display. As a city or county manager, your walk down the hallway is a signal. Your silence in a meeting is a statement. Your tone in an email or response in a crisis becomes a lasting impression.

People are always watching—and more importantly, they're interpreting.

Your staff is watching to see if they're protected, supported, and inspired.

Your elected officials are watching to gauge loyalty, alignment, or resistance.

The public is watching, even when they're silent, especially when they are.

And your critics? They're always watching, waiting to exploit missteps, even imagined ones.

And sometimes, the people who are watching the closest are the very people you trusted the most. Sabotage doesn't always come from enemies—it can come from allies, or those who you thought were. This is why presence, awareness, and emotional control are vital. If you're not tuned in, the subtle acts of disloyalty, ego, or manipulation will move unchecked around you. And you won't even see it coming—until it's too late.

But here's the hard truth: You cannot lead effectively if you've already left emotionally. You need to have a level of empathy as you manage and lead.

When you begin to disengage—whether you're counting the days to retirement or numbing out from political fatigue—you create a power vacuum. Staff sense it. Electeds sense it. Opportunists exploit it. And it becomes the very thing that will end your tenure sooner than expected.

You must remain present—mentally, emotionally, physically.

Because the moment you stop actively leading, you begin quietly surrendering.

That's why legacy isn't just about what you've built, it's about how you finish.

Do you still show up for your team? Are you still mentoring and succession planning?

Are you still giving credit publicly and taking responsibility privately?

Are you still walking the departments and engaging with every level of staff?

Because people remember what you do in the final stretch.

They remember how you treated others.

They remember whether you protected the organization or prioritized your ego.

They remember whether you used your platform to empower—or punish.

And they'll talk about you long after you're gone. Not the headlines, not the salary, not even the title—but how you made them feel, what you stood for, and whether they could trust you when it counted.

So don't take shortcuts in your final chapters. Don't confuse silence for strategy. Don't let fatigue turn into vulnerability. And never forget: a weak leader tries to disappear behind the title. A strong leader stands tall even when the winds shift.

Lead like they're watching—because they are.　But more importantly—lead like someone is learning from you. Because they are too.

◆ **Chapter 11 Summary**

Leadership isn't just about managing tasks—it's about navigating people, personalities, and politics with purpose and integrity. You will face sabotage, ego, and hidden agendas—even from those you trust. But your response defines your legacy. Stay engaged. Stay

present. Lead visibly. Finish strong. Because they're not just watching—some are waiting, and others are learning.

Chapter 12: The Community

As a city manager, you are responsible not just for maintaining a community—but for shaping its future. That future must reflect a delicate balance between honoring the people who have built the city over generations and preparing it to thrive for the generations yet to come. This is the tension between *quality of being* and *quality of life*.

Both matter deeply. And both are your responsibility.

Quality of Being: Don't Forget Where You Came From

Cities grow. Populations shift. Services expand. But in the middle of all that progress is a group of people who often get overlooked: the long-term residents who helped shape the community long before you ever showed up.

These are the people who remember when there was one grocery store, when the annual parade had fifteen floats and ended at the local high school, and when the city's identity wasn't just found in zoning codes and budget documents—but in porch conversations, handshakes at the coffee shop, and Saturday morning ballgames.

This is where Quality of Being comes in. It's the soul of a community: the unspoken values, history, and traditions that make a place feel like home. It's not something you can build with a grant or pave over with a capital improvement plan. It's the thread that connects generations to place.

These residents may not always speak the language of economic development or strategic plans. But they know what the community feels like when it's right—and more importantly, they know when it's starting to feel off. If you don't engage them early, frequently, and respectfully, you risk losing the trust of the people who've carried the city this far.

Remember: change is difficult for everyone, and sometimes people are unable to adapt. It is up to you to communicate this. Not just what's happening, but why. Let them know how new projects still respect the past. Listen when they express concern about the pace of growth or the shift in identity. Explain the purpose behind decisions in terms they relate to. That's where leadership lives—in understanding that not everyone opposes change because they're stubborn or backward-thinking. Sometimes they're grieving the loss of a place they no longer recognize.

It's your job not only to hear that—but to respond with empathy, clarity, and consistency.

Too many managers make the mistake of being so future-focused that they forget who's still living in the present. The temptation is real: modernize, streamline, attract. But if you lose the core of the community in the process, you've gained nothing.

Quality of Being is your anchor. It's the principle that says: no matter how far we grow, we still know who we are. And we don't abandon the people who got us here. In fact, we honor them—not with words or plaques alone, but with policies, presence, and participation.

Quality of Life: Build for Who's Coming Next

While honoring your community's roots is essential, leadership also means preparing for what—and who—is to come. That's the heart of Quality of Life: ensuring your city or town remains livable, vibrant, and competitive in a world that's constantly changing.

This isn't about erasing the past. It's about building a future with intention. A thriving community must offer more than just stability—it must offer opportunity, growth, and a reason for people to stay or move in.

That means making decisions today that may not fully pay off until years—or decades—down the road. It means laying the groundwork for infrastructure that supports tomorrow's residents, not just today's. It means embracing diversity in housing, transit, culture, business, recreation, and technology. You're not just planning for next year's budget, you're planning for someone's future home, someone's first job, someone's sense of belonging.

Remember: you are building for the future, long after you are gone, and for people who are not there yet—people you will never meet. That realization should be both humbling and invigorating. You're helping shape a community for someone's future children, someone's retirement, someone's dream. What greater purpose is there in public service than that?

This is where your excitement must show. Your vision must expand beyond the council chambers and into the horizon. Talk to developers, business leaders, school superintendents, healthcare providers. Ask what tomorrow looks like and what today must do to prepare. Don't be afraid to advocate for projects that challenge the status quo— especially if they improve quality of life for those still finding their way here.

And make sure you define "quality of life" broadly. For some, it's walkable neighborhoods and good restaurants. For others, it's strong schools, safe streets, access to jobs, clean parks, or reliable public transit. It's not one thing—it's many things, working together to create a place where people feel they can build a life.

You must also consider your messaging. How do you make long-term residents feel secure while explaining that growth isn't the enemy— it's the result of a community that others now want to be part of? How do you make prospective residents or businesses see the potential without over-promising or compromising values?

Quality of Life is not about flashy PR—it's about meaningful substance. It's the cumulative effect of policy, design, leadership, and community engagement that says: "We thought about you before you arrived, and we're ready for you."

The Balance: Leading With Both Lenses

As a public executive, your success lies not in choosing between *Quality of Being* or *Quality of Life*, but in learning to lead with an eye on both, simultaneously. That is the true mark of a balanced, thoughtful, and visionary leader.

Quality of Being ensures that no one is left behind. It's your connection to the people who've lived in the community for decades, who raised families there, built businesses there, served on local committees, and remember when City Hall had only one floor. These residents are the backbone of your city's identity. They deserve to be seen, respected, and considered in every decision you make. Ignoring them isn't just poor politics, it's poor leadership. The stability of your city depends on your ability to keep these foundational voices engaged, even as change unfolds around them.

At the same time, Quality of Life demands that you look forward. That you lead with energy, creativity, and urgency in building for future generations. This means making room for growth—not just physical space, but mental and emotional space to welcome new families, businesses, ideas, and cultures. It's about designing systems and communities that will support residents you'll never meet—but who will one day call your city "home."

This is the tension you must hold—leading for who's here now while building for who's coming next. You must honor the story already written while writing the next chapter with courage.

To do this well, you must master the art of presence and projection. Be present enough to understand your community's fears, needs, and concerns today. But also project far enough into the future that you're making decisions that serve the long arc of your city's destiny. That means:

- Walking the neighborhoods of both legacy residents and new subdivisions.

- Listening to those who've lived through past changes and those who are just now arriving.

- Advocating for progress while defending heritage.

- Explaining that growth is not erasure—it's a continuation of community strength.

You must also communicate clearly and often. Let the public know your "why." Show them how you are both preserving and progressing. Use real stories and real people to illustrate how your policies serve both the 30-year resident and the young couple moving in next month.

And above all—be intentional. Because when you lose sight of either lens, your leadership falters. A city built only for the past becomes stagnant. A city built only for the future becomes soulless. But a city led with both vision and reverence becomes something rare: sustainable, inclusive, and truly alive.

Communicate the Why

If leadership is about vision, communication is the vehicle that delivers it. And in city management, over-communication is not just helpful—it's essential. Your ability to explain not just what is happening, but *why* it's happening, is the difference being seen as a bureaucrat versus a true community leader.

When change is coming—whether it's a rezoning, a new subdivision, a tax policy, or a long-term capital project—people are going to react. Some will be excited. Others will be confused or upset. Most will simply not understand the full picture unless you give it to them. And even when you do, the reaction may still be critical—but at least it's informed criticism.

That's why communicating the *why* behind your decisions is your most powerful tool.

But that doesn't mean saying the same thing to everyone in the same way.

Every group in your ecosystem—elected officials, staff, and the community at large—needs the same core message, but it must be tailored in both language and depth.

With your elected officials, you need to go deep.

Give them the full context, data, timelines, policy implications, financial impact, and the potential risks and benefits. This level of detail gives them confidence to support you and defend the decision publicly. If you give them a vague overview, they'll either fill in the blanks with their own assumptions or they'll feel blindsided later when the community pushes back.

With your staff, focus on clarity and relevance.

Show them how this decision or direction impacts their work, their departments, their roles. Be transparent, but also efficient. They don't need a policy thesis—they need to know what it means for operations, logistics, and service delivery. Speak plainly and consistently.

With the community, you must walk a careful line.

The public deserves honesty, but not an information overload. When you give too much detail, especially technical or bureaucratic detail— you open the door to a flood of questions, criticism, and misinformation. Communicate the purpose, the benefit, and the impact. Keep it understandable, relatable, and focused on how it affects their daily lives. Don't bury the message in complexity.

Above all, don't assume once is enough. Repetition is reputation. Communicate early, clearly, and often. Use every platform you have—council meetings, newsletters, website updates, social media, town halls. And be consistent across all channels. Even if people don't agree with your direction, they'll respect your transparency if they understand the rationale.

And remember—tone matters. Communicating the *why* isn't just about facts. It's about showing that you care, that you've thought it through, and that you're listening in return.

Ultimately, people want to feel included in the journey. They want to be told the truth, and they want to know you're not making decisions in a vacuum. So, don't be afraid to over-communicate. Just make sure you're saying the right thing, the right way, to the right people.

That's how you lead with both vision and trust.

Create Legacy Through Inclusion

True legacy in city management is not defined by a groundbreaking ceremony or a final vote tally. It's built on the people you brought along with you, the voices you included, and the trust you cultivated across years of service. Projects will age, plaques will tarnish—but the relationships you build through inclusion will endure.

You are not just leading a city into the future—you're stewarding the present for *everyone*. That means making intentional space for the longtime residents who remember when City Hall was a trailer, and the young professionals arriving with laptops and new expectations. It means inviting in the people who feel unseen and unheard, and making decisions that reflect a mosaic of experiences—not just the loudest or most visible few.

Inclusion is not a box to check—it's the soil where your legacy will grow.

That starts with being present. Show up in every part of the community, not just the ones where you're comfortable. Go to senior centers, youth events, HOA meetings, food banks, churches, local barbershops. The more you show up, the more doors you open. And don't just listen—*invite* feedback. Even when it's hard. Even when it's critical. Especially when it's different from your own view.

When people feel heard, they begin to trust. And when people trust, they begin to support.

Legacy isn't just what you build, it's who you build with.

You'll often face the pressure to prioritize the voices with money, influence, or connections. But your job is to represent the whole. Don't let the desire for quick wins or political favor pull you away from the broader community. It's easy to cut a ribbon in front of a cheering crowd. It's harder to sit down with someone who feels left behind—but *that's where the real work lives*.

This is also where you create future leaders. Inclusion means not just hearing people—it means preparing them. Bringing in new voices to your advisory boards. Encouraging staff to speak up in meetings. Identifying community members who could be tomorrow's councilmembers or city managers—and mentoring them. Your legacy isn't secured by holding the spotlight. It's solidified by passing the torch.

And remember, inclusion must span your entire organization. Staff morale, innovation, and culture all stem from whether people feel seen and valued. You need input from maintenance crews, finance clerks, IT techs, and engineers, not just department heads. They carry institutional knowledge and real-world insight that can't be found in reports or PowerPoint slides.

You're not building a city for one kind of person. You're building for the child growing up here now, the immigrant family arriving next year, the retiree who's lived here for four decades, and the entrepreneur looking to invest. If you leave someone out, you leave potential behind.

So, include boldly. Include often. Include with purpose.

Your greatest legacy won't be a building, a policy, or a budget surplus. It will be the community that believes it was built *with* them—not just *around* them.

Final Thought: Build Forward, Remember Back

Leading a community isn't about choosing between past and future, tradition and innovation, or legacy and growth. It's about embracing the full spectrum—*the quality of being* and *the quality of life*—and managing both with clarity, compassion, and vision.

The greatest mistake a city manager can make is believing their job is to pick a side: that they must either protect what was or chase what could be. But leadership is not a binary act. It is a balancing act—a constant calibration of values, voices, and vision.

You must protect the soul of your city. The people who've raised families here, who've served on PTA boards, who've run the local hardware store for decades. Their stories matter. Their discomfort with rapid change is real. And you must honor that—not out of obligation, but out of gratitude. Their sacrifices helped build the foundation you now stand on.

But at the same time, your job is to prepare for the future. To welcome new families, foster economic development, and build systems and spaces that will serve people you'll never meet. The next generation is counting on you to build a city that works—*not just now*, but twenty years from now.

That's why the most important tool you carry is communication. And the most important lens you look through is empathy.

Explain the "why" behind your decisions—not just once, but consistently. Tailor your messages for different audiences. Give your elected officials deep policy context and long-term implications. Give staff clarity and vision to rally behind. Give your community honesty and transparency without overwhelming them with technical detail that creates fear or opposition. The message is the same—but how you deliver it determines whether people trust it.

This is how cities move forward—by bringing everyone with them, not leaving some behind.

So, as you manage budgets, draft strategic plans, or speak at ribbon cuttings, remember: You're not just building sidewalks and sewer lines. You're building belonging. You're protecting the heart of a city while expanding its reach. You're the bridge between memory and momentum.

Don't be afraid to honor where you came from.

Don't hesitate to build for those who haven't arrived yet.

And don't forget—the best cities live in both places.

That's the leadership your community needs.

That's the legacy your leadership can leave behind.

◆ Chapter 12 Summary

True leadership balances respect for long-standing residents and traditions while building boldly for a future you may never see. Honor the community's identity, communicate with clarity, and lead with both vision and empathy. Cities aren't either-or—they're both-and. Build belonging as you build progress.

Chapter 13: Never Say No

As a leader, your words carry weight—often more than you realize. And one of the heaviest words you can use is "No." To staff, it can shut down innovation. To the community, it can signal disregard. To elected officials, it can sound like resistance. That's why, in local government leadership, one of the most powerful strategies you can adopt is simple: Try never to say no.

This isn't about being agreeable to a fault. It doesn't mean surrendering to every request or turning a blind eye to bad ideas. What it means is that you approach situations with curiosity rather than judgment—that you lead with possibility, not finality.

It's easy to say no. But the real strength lies in helping others see better options without crushing their confidence or disengaging them from the process.

Guiding Staff Without Discouraging Them

Leadership is about development. And one of the most valuable things you can do as a manager is help your team grow—not just in skill, but in confidence and perspective.

When a staff member brings you a recommendation—even one that's incomplete, misaligned, or just not the right fit—don't start with critique. Start with inquiry. Ask:

- "Have you considered what might happen if this part changed?"

- "What if we tested this idea on a smaller scale first?"

- "What might the public say about this if we rolled it out tomorrow?"

Give them something to take back and reframe, rather than reject. Let them own the path forward. This builds trust and fuels creativity.

The point isn't to be soft. It's to be strategic. If you immediately tell someone their idea won't work, you've shut the door. But if you invite them to reimagine it, you've opened a whole new hallway.

Remember—staff want to be part of solutions. And as their leader, you need to fuel their momentum, not flatten it.

Serving the Community Beyond the Loudest Voice

In public service, one of the hardest things to explain is that you don't serve individual voices—you serve the entire community. The loudest voice in the room may only represent a sliver of the population, but if you say "no" to them outright, you risk alienation, misinformation, and public distrust.

Instead of "No," try:

- "Let's look into this further and come back with a full response."

- "There are other factors involved here that we'll need to balance."

- "We're taking all views into consideration—yours included— as we form a recommendation."

You're not dodging. You're deliberating. You're not giving in— you're governing.

Community members won't always have the full story. They're not supposed to. That's why you're in the seat you're in. But they want to be heard, and they want to believe their input matters. That starts by how you respond.

And sometimes, that means you don't respond at all—at least not right away. Give space, gather facts, let emotions cool, and then return with facts, clarity, and compassion.

Don't mistake volume for value. Don't allow one person's outrage to define your direction. And never forget—you are here for everyone, including those who didn't show up that night at the podium.

Understanding the Role of the Elected Body

One of the most misunderstood dynamics in local government is this: you may be executing a policy or action you don't personally support. That's not failure. That's governance.

You work for the governing body. And sometimes, the public doesn't understand that. You're the face of the action, even if it was their vote, their direction, and their motion that got it there.

This is where restraint matters. You don't throw your board under the bus. You don't say "Well, this wasn't my idea." Instead, you own the implementation while still maintaining your integrity.

When you must push back, do it privately—with precision, with professionalism, and with possible alternatives.

And when you must say no—because sometimes you will—don't let it be the first word out of your mouth. Explore. Suggest. Redirect. Ask. Reframe. Let them feel your investment in the process even if the outcome won't go their way.

That's the distinction between managing and leading.

Final Thought: Redirection Is Stronger Than Rejection

True leadership balances respect for long-standing residents and traditions while building boldly for a future you may never see. You can't please everyone. You won't always agree. But how you respond—especially when you don't agree—will define your character and your influence.

The community you serve is not just made up of complaints, emails, and public comment cards. It's people—some who have lived there for decades, and others who haven't arrived yet. And you are leading for all of them.

Don't let fear make your decisions. Don't let fatigue do your talking. And never let your first instinct be "No."

Because most of the time, what people really want is someone to say:

"Let's figure this out."

◆ Chapter 13 Summary

Don't shut down ideas—reframe them. Great leadership isn't about saying no; it's about creating momentum by guiding staff, engaging the community with care, and implementing policy with professionalism. Redirect. Reimagine. Respond—with vision.

Chapter 14: When You're Used, Abused, and Thrown to the Curb

Recovering from Betrayal and Political Fallout

Leadership in public service often comes with a silent clause—that your integrity will be tested, and sometimes even discarded, not because of who you are, but because of what you represent. You're the professional. The adult in the room. The bearer of hard truths and unpopular realities. But when politics shift, when agendas change, when your usefulness expires—you may find yourself cast aside.

This is the part no one prepares you for.

This is when your integrity matters—and you have to ask yourself, "What is it worth?" When everything you built is questioned or deconstructed. When your service, your loyalty, and your effort are no longer reciprocated. You may feel betrayed, humiliated, and even discarded. But how you respond in these moments will define your legacy far more than any ribbon-cutting or council presentation ever could.

The Anatomy of a Fall

It doesn't always start with confrontation. Often, it's silence. A meeting you're no longer invited to. A request you made that now goes unacknowledged. A slow retreat of trust from the people who once relied on you.

Other times it's sudden—a closed-session meeting, a public statement, a social media storm. One day you're in control, the next you're watching the narrative about you being written by others.

It's brutal. It's disorienting. It's deeply personal.

You may have been the glue holding the team together. The leader who brought the organization through a crisis. The stabilizing force that shielded elected officials from their own missteps. And yet, now, you are painted as the problem. Or worse, made to feel irrelevant.

This is when the loneliness of leadership becomes real. You realize how quickly people can pivot. How allies become bystanders. How justifications are made at your expense.

But here's the truth: you are not alone. Many of us have been there. And survival—let alone recovery—starts with this understanding.

What You Learn When It All Falls Apart

In the aftermath of betrayal or fallout, a strange kind of clarity emerges. It's painful, but it's pure. You are reminded of who people truly are. You learn who shows up for you when there's nothing left to gain—and who quietly disappears, hoping not to be associated with your fall.

You'll find that the circle you thought surrounding you is smaller than you imagined. But that's not a loss. It's a reveal.

If you survive a major fallout and still have your job—or even if you don't—remember this: you will quickly discover who your true colleagues and friends are, because they will stand beside you in the storm. They'll call. They'll check in. They'll grab a cup of coffee and say, "You okay?" They won't ask for details, and they won't disappear. These people are your compass going forward.

But also, be prepared for those who distanced themselves in the chaos to try to return once the dust settles. Know this—and remember it. Their return may be transactional, not relational. And while you don't need to burn every bridge, you do need to take note of who ran when you needed them most. Leadership requires trust, and trust needs to be earned—again, and sometimes never again.

You'll also learn what parts of the job were truly meaningful and what parts were merely ego. Titles vanish. Authority fades. But how you treated people, how you led with—or without—integrity, and how you faced the fire will follow you into every room you enter next.

This is where your real character is forged—not in the comfort of a well-run council meeting, but in the fallout of one gone sideways. You'll learn what you're made of. You'll realize that survival isn't the end goal—resilience is. And moving forward with clarity, courage, and character is what truly matters.

The Dangerous Allure of Bitterness

Anger is a natural response to betrayal. So is bitterness. But when it becomes your identity, it will quietly sabotage your future.

You may be tempted to speak your truth publicly, to name names, to "set the record straight." But be cautious. While truth matters, timing and tone matter more. You may feel vindicated in the moment, but the long-term consequences can cost you your reputation, future opportunities, or peace of mind.

Bitterness poisons your memory. It rewrites your accomplishments with cynicism and leaves you replaying conversations like war games. It robs you of closure.

Instead, channel your energy into healing and rebuilding. Write down your experience—not to share, but to process. Talk to someone neutral. Go for long walks. Work out. Sleep. Let yourself grieve the loss of your role, your work family, your position. That grief is real.

But don't let it become your story.

Recovering Without Retaliating

One of the most powerful things you can do after a fall is to refuse to retaliate. That doesn't mean you forget. It doesn't mean you let people off the hook. It means you choose dignity.

When people ask what happened, choose your words carefully. Don't lie—but don't let bitterness write your script. Tell them you served with integrity, and you moved on when the time came. Let others say what they will. The people who matter will look at your history and your conduct—not the noise around your departure.

And remember, people are always watching. Your next employer, your next team, even your next set of elected officials will take notice of how you handled adversity.

Your rebound is your revenge. Your silence can speak volumes.

And when it comes to the press or even email inquiries about your well-being, resist the urge to respond—no matter how tempting it may be. Don't write statements. Don't offer clarity. Don't try to correct the record. The people who genuinely care about you will text or call to talk. They will want to hear your voice, not read your words through a filtered lens. The press is not your friend, no matter how kind the email may sound. And what you say will never be printed exactly as you mean it.

Your words will be trimmed, twisted, or taken out of context—used in ways that do not serve your healing, your legacy, or your future. Preserve your peace by protecting your narrative. You don't owe the public your pain, and you certainly don't owe anyone your defense.

Let your professionalism speak for itself. Let your quiet resolve do the talking. That is not weakness—it's restraint. And in times of political fallout, restraint is a rare and powerful kind of strength.

The Truth About Political Fallout

Political fallout is rarely fair. It often has little to do with your performance and everything to do with perception, timing, and optics. You can have a clean record, a trail of successes, and the admiration of your staff—and still be ousted because it served someone else's agenda.

You may be let go without a clear reason. You may be asked to resign under vague accusations. You may even be the scapegoat for a mistake you didn't make. And the hardest part? The silence. The people who once praised you, stood beside you, or cheered your accomplishments may go quiet. Not because they agree with what happened, but because they don't want to be caught in the crossfire.

And that's the truth of political fallout—you will often suffer it alone.

Don't let yourself believe that everyone will care about what happened to you. The reality is only a few will. Most people will stay silent and move on with their lives, especially if acknowledging your situation puts them at risk. While you may be sitting still, emotionally or professionally wounded, waiting for consolation or public defense from the community or your elected officials, that moment may never come.

The people who truly know you, your character, and your contribution—they're the ones who will reach out. They will call, text, or show up. And that small group will mean more than a hundred empty statements or performative posts online. Don't measure your value by the number of people who speak up publicly. Measure it by the few who stand by you privately.

Your integrity, the work you've done, and the way you recover, that's what will define you, not the silence of others.

Final Thought: Integrity Is the Only Job You'll Always Have

There will be moments in your career when the very people you've supported, defended, and sacrificed will walk away from you. Some will go quietly. Others may cheer your downfall. But what will hurt most, what feels like a stronger betrayal, that will come from those who know better.

But this is the moment your integrity matters most. This is when you ask yourself: *What is my integrity worth?* If your answer is "everything," then you've already won—regardless of the outcome.

You may not be able to control how others respond to your fallout. But you can control your posture. You can walk with your head held high, not because everything went right, but because you stayed grounded in who you are. You didn't retaliate. You didn't burn the organization you worked so hard to establish. You absorbed the blow, or blows, with grace—and that's what real leadership looks like.

As noted throughout this book, you learn, painfully but clearly, who your true colleagues and friends are. If you survive and stay on the job, or if you're forced to step away, those who sincerely care about you will reach out. They'll check on you. They'll offer help, words of encouragement, or just space to breathe. Those who never really supported you? Well, they will continue to stay silent. Some may even return later, when they feel doing so won't negatively impact their own career. Always remember who stood by you when it mattered most. That's the gift beneath the pain.

Don't respond to the press. Don't respond to angling emails asking how you're doing. Those that truly care will call, text, or show up. The press is not your friend—and no matter how carefully you choose your words, they'll never print what you truly meant. Let your silence speak volumes and protect your future.

Lastly, know this: your story isn't over. Fallout is a chapter, not the book. You may feel discarded, but you are not done. Use this time to reflect, heal, rebuild, and reconnect with what matters. Let the betrayal sharpen your wisdom, not your cynicism.

You've built too much, cared too deeply, and led too many to be defined by one bad ending. So, stand tall—even when they walk away. Especially when they walk away.

Because how you carry yourself in silence will echo longer than any headline ever could.

◆ Chapter 14 Summary

Betrayal and political fallout are inevitable in public leadership—but how you respond defines your legacy. When others walk away, your integrity, presence, and emotional control must stand tall. Protect your voice, preserve your dignity, and always remember those who truly care will show up. Let the silence reveal who's real. Fallout is not your finale—it's the forge that shapes the leader you become next.

Chapter 15: Gotcha Moments

There's a unique breed of moment in public service—a moment that's quick, sharp, and highly visible. It may last five minutes in real time, but it lingers forever in memory, on the record, and across careers. These are the "gotcha moments." They're born from ambushes at the dais, unexpected public accusations, or perfectly timed media stings. The five minutes of fame also pertains to how some elected officials like to blindside staff or other elected officials on the dais when the public is watching. Whether driven by ego, strategy, or pure politics, they're engineered for impact—and you, as a manager, are often the one left holding the damage.

These moments are often less about facts and more about perception. And in government, perception is power. A comment taken out of context, a question sprung without warning, or a reaction caught on camera—each can be amplified far beyond its original scope.

If you haven't faced one yet, you will. And how you prepare for, respond to, and recover from these moments will determine not just your career longevity—but your credibility.

Ambushes Aren't Accidents

The first thing to remember is this: most gotcha moments aren't spontaneous. They're scripted and prepared well in advance – don't let anyone tell you otherwise.

When an elected official "suddenly" asks a controversial question during a council meeting, or a member of the public levels a harsh accusation during public comment, it's often pre-planned. These moments are designed to catch you off guard—while cameras are rolling and an audience is tuned in.

The tactic is simple: create discomfort and force a public reaction. It's not about getting the right answer; it's about creating the rightimpression. And often, it's done for political gain—especially during election seasons or budget negotiations.

You may be tempted to match the drama with a sharp defense or a bold correction. Resist the urge. In that moment, your demeanor will speak louder than your words.

Stay composed. Take a breath. If necessary, defer the answer by saying, "I'd be happy to follow up with a detailed response." That one sentence does more than stall—it protects. It protects the integrity of the information, the dignity of the process, and your own emotional composure.

Everyone Remembers the Reaction

In a gotcha moment, no one remembers the actual question—they remember your response. The response lingers also forever in memory, on the record, and across your career.

Did you look rattled? Defensive? Did your voice rise? Did you flinch?

People assess your credibility and confidence not just by what you say—but how you say it when you're under fire. These moments reveal your leadership presence. Or expose its absence.

That's why you must train yourself to expect the unexpected. Role-play with your team. Anticipate hot-button issues. Prepare statements in advance for controversial projects or personnel matters. And always walk into public meetings with the mindset that something could happen. Not because you're paranoid—but because you're prepared.

The Staff Collateral

When gotcha moments target your staff, the stakes are even higher.

It's one thing to defend yourself, it's another to be expected to answer for a department head, a line employee, or an incident that's already been sensationalized in the public eye. This is where your leadership shows.

Take responsibility in public. Never pass the blame down. Never say, "That's not my department," or "That's not my issue." Instead, say, "We're aware of the concern, and I'll work with our team to address it directly." Then follow through.

Privately, you can address staff accountability. Publicly, you shield your team from humiliation. This builds trust, protects morale, and reinforces a culture where your people know you won't abandon them when things get rough.

What the Public Really Wants

The audience for these moments isn't just the person behind the microphone, it's the community watching from home, the stakeholders reading the news story, and the staff taking mental notes.

They're watching to see how you lead.

But more importantly—they're watching to see if you fail.

That's the real truth. In today's world of viral clips and instant judgment, the public doesn't just consume leadership, they scrutinize it. They observe with a quiet, often skeptical eye, waiting to see whether you'll crack, stumble, overreact, or expose weakness under pressure. This isn't cynicism—it's human nature. People want to know if the person entrusted with managing their city, their budget, their quality of life, can really stand tall when the spotlight burns the hottest.

And for some, that curiosity leans more toward hope than support. Not everyone watching is rooting for you. Some are waiting for a headline. Others want justification for their criticism. A few just enjoy the spectacle of someone else squirming in the hot seat. You must accept this without bitterness—and lead despite it.

The public doesn't expect perfection—but they do expect poise. They want to know that the person at the helm of their city or county can weather pressure without lashing out, melting down, or hiding behind vague answers. They want to see confidence without arrogance, clarity without condescension, and humility without weakness.

So when the moment comes, don't just think about the person trying to corner you. Think about the hundreds or thousands of others— some silent, some skeptical—who are watching you navigate it. You're not just managing a moment. You're modeling leadership.

Media Will Only Show the Clip That Sells

You may think handled the moment well. You may think stood your ground, answered with grace, and navigated the situation perfectly. But the media? They don't care about the full exchange—they care about the most clickable ten seconds.

The press isn't paid to capture nuance. They're paid to capture attention. And attention lives in the headline, the pull quote, the freeze frame that makes you look surprised or frustrated, or the soundbite taken out of context. You could spend twenty minutes walking through a thoughtful explanation of a sensitive topic, only to have the story reduce it to: *"City Manager Defends Controversial Decision Amid Public Outcry."*

The reality is this: the media is going to write the story the way they want. They sell papers, clicks, ad space—for a reason. The caption is what captures the reader, not the context. Their business model is built around attention, not accuracy. That means they will say and write what they want, with or without your commentary, clarification, or correction.

So, most of the time—not all the time, but most—it's best not to engage with the media in the heat of the moment. Don't rush to issue a rebuttal, don't respond emotionally to a misquote, and don't expect the full truth to make the evening news or tomorrow's headline. You'll only be hurting yourself, giving more airtime to something that should have passed quickly, and potentially adding fuel to a fire that wasn't really burning until you fanned it.

The more you address the issue or problem, the longer the story lives. Every follow-up statement, every correction, every attempt to set the record straight gives the media a reason to continue the narrative. You may think you're providing clarity, but in their world, you're keeping the controversy alive. Sometimes silence isn't weakness—it's strategy.

This doesn't mean you avoid the media entirely. It means you use discernment. Choose when to speak, and more importantly, choose when silence serves you better. When you do respond, be measured, be factual, and be brief. Let others, your staff, elected officials, or community partners—speak to your credibility when appropriate. Your best defense isn't always your voice, it's your record, your consistency, and your long game.

When the media only shows the clip, make sure your character is what fills in the rest.

Protecting Yourself Without Losing Yourself

It's easy to become jaded in leadership—especially when you've been blindsided, misrepresented, or made the subject of someone else's two-minute performance. Your natural instinct will be to retreat, tighten your circle, pull back from staff, and operate in a shell of protection. That's understandable. But it's also dangerous.

The moment you stop trusting anyone, you stop being effective.

You cannot lead from behind a wall of paranoia—but you also can't pretend the hallway is safe when it's not. That's the paradox of leadership: protecting yourself without losing yourself.

What does that mean in practice?

It means remaining available but not exposed. Approachable, but not naïve. It means you still walk the departments, still listen to concerns, still meet with residents—but you don't share every detail of your thoughts, plans, or vulnerabilities with people who haven't earned that trust.

It means understanding the difference between being transparent and being reckless.

It also means you learn to control the narrative with your actions, not your explanations. You don't respond to every critic. You don't try to defend yourself against every accusation in the press. You don't spend hours rehashing your version of events in meetings or emails. Instead, you keep doing the job, the right way, with integrity and calm. Because over time, your consistency speaks louder than any rumor ever will.

This is also where preparation matters. Keep your documentation tight. Save your calendars, your emails, your notes. When the time comes to defend a decision, let the record do the talking. You are not protecting yourself with paranoia, you are doing so with professionalism. Have your receipts, but don't lead with them.

And most importantly, don't let the moment change you so much that you forget why you started.

You started this work because you care. You wanted to build something. You wanted to serve. And while not everyone around you may respect that, you must never lose sight of your mission.

Remember: you are not the job. You are not the title. Those can be taken, tossed, or smeared. But your values, your dignity, and your way of treating others—even in the worst moments—are yours to protect.

So protect yourself. But don't lose yourself.

Because no matter what storm you're in, someone else is watching how you weather it. And the example you set today may be the courage someone else needs tomorrow.

Final Thought: The Moment Will Pass—The Memory Will Not

The worst day of your professional life may last five minutes in real time, but its consequences can echo for years. The footage, the headlines, the awkward silence in the meeting—they don't define your career, but they can shape how people perceive it.

What matters most is how you respond.

If you let one ambush destroy your confidence, if you internalize a single headline as your entire story, or if you allow one grandstanding elected official to fracture your purpose, you're surrendering far more than the moment—you're surrendering your leadership.

But if you stay composed, stay grounded, and stay true to the mission, the moment will pass. And how you handled it—how you kept your dignity, protected your staff, led with grace—that's what they'll remember.

Because even in the darkest leadership moments, people are still watching. And not just your critics—your team is watching. Your future is watching. And someone else who's learning how to lead is watching, too.

Remember that these moments don't just expose the cracks in others, they reveal the strength in you.

Your job is to keep showing up, keep leading forward, and keep the long view in sight. The news cycle will move on. The rumors will fade. The public will forget. But the way you carried yourself—that's what will live in memory.

Lead like the moment matters, but live like your legacy is bigger than that moment.

Because it is.

"Gotcha" moments may only last five minutes—but the consequences can last a lifetime. Whether it's a surprise attack in a meeting, a misleading headline, or a public stumble, your response defines your character more than the moment does. Don't chase the spotlight, and don't fight shadows. Stay grounded, protect your team, lead with dignity, and remember: your legacy is built on how you carry yourself when others hope you'll fall.

Chapter 16: The Quiet Power of Consistency

Why showing up, doing the work, and staying steady builds more trust than any title or speech.

In a world that values headlines and highlight reels, it's easy to overlook the most powerful trait in leadership: consistency. It doesn't make news. It doesn't stir applause. But in public management, it's what earns respect, reinforces stability, and keeps your organization moving forward when everything around you is shifting.

Consistency is what people come to rely on—not your title, not your charisma, not your ability to speak into a microphone. What truly builds trust is when people know what they can expect from you. It's showing up, following through, treating people fairly, and not letting emotions or politics dictate your every move.

In local government, where public scrutiny is high and pressure comes from all directions, consistency isn't just a trait—it's a survival skill.

Leadership Is Often Boring on Purpose

The truth is, good leadership can be boring. That's not an insult—that's a compliment. Predictability in leadership is a form of emotional safety. When staff know what version of you is going to walk in the door, they can do their jobs better. When elected officials know you won't flip based on who complains the loudest, they trust your guidance. When the public sees a steady hand at the wheel, they feel stability.

You don't need to be the entertainer or add commentary - you need to be dependable. That's what separates leaders who last from those who flame out.

However, don't confuse consistency with inaction. You can be bold in ideas and steady in behavior. You can advocate for innovation without being erratic. And you can make tough decisions while maintaining a calm, fair process. The most effective managers are the ones who understand that steadiness doesn't mean stagnation—it means control.

You Can't Be Everything—But You Must Be Consistent

You'll hear this phrase a lot: "You can't please everyone." It's true. In fact, if you're doing your job right, someone is most likely mad at you. But the counterbalance to that is being fair, and being known for how you make decisions, not just what decisions you make.

You won't win every vote on the dais. You won't gain applause from every neighborhood. But you can build a reputation for being methodical, open, honest, and reliable.

Staff will respect you more if you're consistent with expectations, regardless of who is in the room. Don't play favorites. Don't change your standards based on personalities. Be consistent in how you discipline, how you recognize good work, and how you engage with employees at all levels. That doesn't mean being robotic—but it means being fair.

Your community doesn't need you to be flashy. They need you to be faithful—to the work, to the people, and to the process.

Consistency Is Your Best Political Strategy

Politics is inherently unstable. Elections come and go. Board compositions change. And agendas shift with the wind. But your job isn't to chase popularity—it's to provide institutional memory, guidance, and continuity.

Consistency is what anchors the organization during political change.

It's easy to get caught up in reacting to new council members or trying to accommodate the latest loud voice at the podium. But bending too much sends a very dangerous message—that your principles are negotiable. That your decisions are based on who's asking, not what's right.

Instead, create a clear and visible decision-making framework. Follow it. Communicate it. Stick to it. Let your actions be your message. And when new electeds come in, introduce them to that framework—not because you're trying to assert power, but because it's your job to protect the process and the people behind it.

Elected officials may not always agree with you, but they'll come to appreciate your steadiness—especially when they've been burned by chaos elsewhere.

The Staff Are Watching Closely

Your employees learn more from what you do or don't do than what you say. If you're inconsistent, they'll become cautious. If you're reactive, they'll become silent. If you make emotional decisions, they'll lose trust.

But if you're consistent—especially in hard times—they will follow you.

That means showing up to the hard conversations. That means being present in the field, not just in meetings. That means responding to problems the same way you respond to praise: with calm, fairness, and focus.

It also means modeling how to act when things go wrong. When a project fails, or a decision draws criticism, your staff will watch how you handle it. Do you assign blame? Do you panic? Or do you calmly assess, redirect, and move forward?

Every reaction, good or bad, is a message. Every moment is a teaching opportunity. Consistency creates a culture of stability, even when circumstances are unstable.

What Consistency Doesn't Mean

Let's be clear—consistency doesn't mean rigidity.

You need to adapt when circumstances change. You need to learn from mistakes. You need to grow as a person and a leader. But your core principles—transparency, fairness, accountability, professionalism—should not change based on who's in front of you.

That's what consistency looks like: flexibility in tools, firmness in values.

And don't mistake consistency for being overly cautious. You can make bold moves. You can try new approaches. But the way you explain them, implement them, and own the outcomes—that's where consistency matters most.

Final Thought: Stability Is Leadership's Greatest Gift

As uncertain as the world is, a consistent leader is a gift to the organization.

It may not make headlines. It may not win awards. But it creates trust, stability, and clarity for those you serve. Over time, people remember who kept things steady when others wavered. They remember who could be counted on—to be present and dependable.

Your legacy as a city or county manager may not be written in the boldest font, but it will be etched into the culture you shaped, the people you mentored, and the organization you steadied.

Be consistent. Be clear. Be calm.

Because that's what real leadership looks like.

Consistency doesn't mean doing the same thing— it means showing up with the same principles. Trust isn't built on brilliance— it's built on stability, fairness, and presence. In a political world full of noise, consistency is your clearest message.

Chapter 17: Elected Officials Are Not Your Friends

Clear-eyed boundaries and protecting your career from blurred lines

There's a hard truth you need to hear, whether you've been in city management for two years or twenty: elected officials are not your friends. They are partners in governance with clearly defined roles.

They may laugh with you, confide in you, invite you to dinner, or even tell you they've got your back when things get tough. But never confuse proximity for friendship. Because one day—without warning—you may find yourself on the other side of a vote, an investigation, or a press conference, wondering what happened to all that trust you worked so hard to gain.

And here's the answer: *Nothing happened to it. It was never there.*

Friendship implies loyalty without condition. Public service is not built on that. Your relationship with elected officials is conditional by design—based on votes, public pressure, shifting alliances, and the needs of the moment. Their loyalty is to their constituents, their platform, and often, their political survival. You just happen to be along for the ride—for as long as you're useful.

Blurred Lines Lead to Broken Trust

The moment you start thinking you're "in" with an elected official you've already lost. It means your judgment is now clouded by favoritism. It means your credibility is at risk with other members of the governing body. And it means your decisions may begin to serve one person's political needs instead of the community's well-being.

Not only is that unethical, it's unsustainable.

Elected officials will test boundaries, sometimes without even realizing it. They'll casually ask for favors, subtly suggesting, "Just take care of this quietly," or ask you to prioritize a pet project over what's in the budget or Capital Improvement Program. If they think you're close, they'll expect latitude. They'll interpret your silence as agreement. And when they cross the line—*and they will*—they'll drag your reputation with them.

The more distance you maintain professionally and personally, the more respect you will command.

Familiarity Is Not Friendship

You will likely spend more time with your mayor or councilmembers than with your family on some weeks. That's part of the job. You'll go to ribbon cuttings, community events, strategy meetings, joint interviews, and even after-hours dinners. That's normal. What's not normal—or safe—is assuming that shared time equals shared loyalty.

They may invite you in to gain your trust—or to keep tabs on you.

They may confide in you about other councilmembers—or test your reactions.

They may treat you like a friend in private—but vote against you in public.

And it will sting. Why? Because you're human.

This mindset protects you *and* them.

The Risk of "Side Conversations"

A particularly dangerous trap is the off-the-record, one-on-one conversations. These seem harmless. A councilmember pulls you aside and says, "Hey, just between us…" or "Don't put this in writing, but…" That's the moment to pause. Because anything said in private—if exposed—will paint you as complicit, biased, or worse, deceitful and untrustworthy.

Side conversations breed suspicion. They may start with small talk, but they often end with misunderstandings or manipulation. If something is worth saying, it's worth saying in the open or in a documented setting.

That doesn't mean you can't have candid discussions. Just imagine how these conversations would sound if played on the news tomorrow because they more likely will be. This approach helps ensure that your words remain respectful and appropriate, even in private settings.

When You're Caught in the Middle

Sometimes your entire governing body is fractured. You'll have factions. One group wants to go in one direction, another wants the opposite—and they both want you to be "on their side." Your job is not to choose a side. Your job is to manage the organization, implement the lawful policies set by the body, and keep the trains running.

But neutrality is not passivity.

You must be firm in your ethics, clear in your processes, and consistent in your behavior. And when challenged, you don't fold to appease a political personality—you stand on policy, procedure, and principle. That's what leadership looks like. It's also what your survival requires.

Don't Mistake Politeness for Trust

One of the most dangerous habits managers fall into is assuming that a cordial relationship means a safe one. A councilmember smiles, praises your performance, compliments your tie—and then votes to terminate your contract. It happens. Often.

That's why you must separate political courtesy from personal connection. It's not cynicism—it's professionalism. You're not there to be liked. You're there to be trusted, respected, and—when necessary—held accountable for your leadership decisions. Keep that as your compass.

Protecting Your Sanity and Your Career

The moment you treat elected officials as friends, your boundaries begin to erode. So protect them:

- Avoid personal gifts or favors. Even small things can look like impropriety.

- Keep text and email exchanges professional and brief. Assume they'll be public one day.

- Don't socialize excessively or privately. Especially not one on one.

- Document decisions and directions. Don't rely on memory or "understandings."

- Be consistent. Treat every elected official the same way—no special access, no special treatment.

Your job is lonely enough. Don't confuse comfort for connection. Find your true friendships outside of the council chambers.

When the Friendship Becomes a Weapon

Sometimes, elected officials will try to use their closeness with you as leverage. You'll hear things like:

- "We already talked about this, didn't we?"

- "Well, the manager agrees with me."

- "Off the record, the manager told me this was already happening."

Whether true or not, these claims can create real damage. Because now your professionalism is in question, your neutrality is doubted, and your standing with other elected officials is fractured. This is why you must protect the boundaries early—and often.

Every relationship with an elected official should be built on three foundations:

- Transparency: Nothing you say in private should contradict what you'll say in public.

- Equity: Every official deserves the same access, same updates, and same respect.

- Process: Let the systems guide the interaction, not personal comfort or favoritism.

These aren't walls—they're guardrails. You can still build rapport. You can still be respectful. But if your relationship with one elected official becomes a vulnerability, it will eventually be weaponized.

When It's Time to Draw the Line

There may come a time when an elected official crosses that line entirely. They might:

- Ask you to do something unethical.

- Try to intimidate or threaten your position.

- Use personal information to gain leverage.

- Harass or bully you or your staff.

In those moments, it is critical to act—not react.

Document everything. Notify your legal counsel. Inform the full board if necessary. And take appropriate action in accordance with your contract, charter, municipal code or organizational policy.

You are not powerless. You are not there to be anyone's pawn. And protecting your staff, your integrity, and the organization itself may require you to stand firm—even if it's unpopular or personally costly.

You cannot lead an ethical organization if you're allowing unethical behavior to continue unchecked, especially from those who govern.

Final Thought: Keep the Line Bright

This chapter is not about paranoia—it's about preparation. It's about being proactive. It's about protecting your credibility and your career from the erosion that starts when boundaries blur. Because once the lines fade, so does the trust. Not just between you and one elected official—but between you and the entire governing body, the public, and your staff.

You were hired to manage, not to be managed.

You were hired to advise, not to be recruited into private agendas.

You were hired to lead, not to pick sides.

So, lead accordingly.

Let your professionalism be what earns their respect, not your proximity. Let your performance speak louder than your alliances. Let your integrity be your shield—because it's the one thing no one can take away from you unless you give it up willingly.

And always remember: Friendship can be a beautiful thing—but in governance, clarity and boundaries are far more valuable.

◆ Chapter 17 Summary

The moment you confuse elected officials for friends, you begin risking your judgment, your objectivity, and your job. Respect the role, protect the boundaries, and serve the entire body—not just one relationship. Professional distance is not coldness—it's the foundation of ethical leadership.

Chapter 18: Why Electeds Run for Office

When it comes to working with elected officials, most city and county managers know the golden rule: manage up, but don't get manipulated. That's easier said than done. The key to navigating those waters effectively is to understand the real motivations behind why someone runs for public office in the first place.

Forget the official campaign platforms for a moment. Ignore the slogans, the smiling yard signs, and the polished speeches. If you want to be an effective executive in government, you need to understand the *person* behind the title. Because their motivation will drive how they govern, how they interact with you, and—most importantly— how they will treat you when things get tough.

In decades past, the motivation for running for office was often altruistic: a deep-rooted desire to give back to the community. That reason still exists—but it's not as common as it once was. Today, the reasons are more varied, more personal, and at times, more self-serving. None of that is inherently wrong but understanding the "why" gives you the upper hand in managing expectations, building relationships, and avoiding political landmines.

So, what are those motivations? They typically fall into eight distinct categories. You'll see variations and combinations of these, but one (or more) usually takes center stage.

---

1. Someone Made Them Angry

This is one of the most dangerous and unpredictable motivations. A resident gets upset over a rezoning decision, a fee increase, or a school boundary change—and decides they're going to "fix it" by running for office. Their campaign is fueled by emotion and aimed at disruption. They may have little interest in governing or collaboration. Their mission is personal and often emotionally charged.

This group also includes a particularly sensitive and problematic subset: former staff members who were terminated or left on bad terms. They come back, not just as critics, but as candidates—determined to "expose the unfairness" they believe they experienced. Often, they carry a sense of personal betrayal and aim to bring turmoil to the city from a position of authority. These situations are particularly challenging because these individuals know your operations, your weaknesses, and how to exploit both public sentiment and media narratives.

These electeds are hard to reason with and often operate with a chip on their shoulder. Their loyalty isn't to the institution—it's to their cause, their agenda, or worse, their vendetta.

As a manager, you'll need to engage with empathy but also establish clear and careful boundaries. Their passion is real, but unchecked emotion can burn bridges and derail progress quickly. Treat them with respect—but lead with caution. Document everything. And always remain composed.

---

2. They Think They Can Do It Better

This one is very common—and subtle. You'll recognize it in the elected official who constantly second-guesses staff, who insists they know "how things really work," and who views city operations like a DIY project.

They've watched from the sidelines, maybe served on a board or committee, and now believe that with just a little common sense and elbow grease, they can fix the whole system.

These officials require patience. Show them the complexity of the job, the data behind the decisions, and the impact of unintended consequences. They're not your enemy—but they can become one if they think you're patronizing them.

Educating them (without embarrassing them) is your best move. Help them realize that leadership is more than just confidence, it's also responsibility.

---

3. It's a Stepping Stone

Some elected officials never plan to stay. They're using the city council or school board as a launching pad for higher office: county supervisor, state representative, even Congress.

Their focus is often more about image than policy. They'll chase headlines, make symbolic gestures, and sometimes grandstand— especially if a camera is nearby.

This doesn't mean they're ineffective, but their timeline is short and their patience is limited. They want wins they can cite on the campaign trail.

Your job here is strategic alignment. Give them opportunities to be seen, but guide them toward efforts that also benefit the organization. Let them claim credit—but ensure the work is solid and sustainable. As Harry S. Truman once said, "It is amazing what you can accomplish if you do not care who gets the credit."

---

4. They Want to Give Back

This is the legacy-driven leader. They care deeply about the community, often because they've lived there for decades, raised their family there, or benefited from its services.

They usually value staff, respect process, and seek consensus. They want to leave the community better than they found it.

These officials are your allies. Nurture that relationship, but don't take it for granted. They're often the voice of reason on contentious issues—and the best defense against more volatile personalities.

---

5. They Want Visibility or an Ego Boost

Let's not sugarcoat this one. Some people run for office to be seen, to be heard, and to be applauded. They want recognition, respect, and control—and the dais is their stage.

You'll see them interrupt staff during meetings, demand credit for ideas they didn't originate, or inject themselves into operational matters they don't understand.

Don't mock or dismiss them—out loud or behind closed doors. Instead, learn how to redirect their energy. Flattery, paired with clear expectations, can go a long way. Give them small wins that allow them to feel important—while steering them away from major disruption.

---

6. They Have a Single-Issue Passion

Whether it's animal control, affordable housing, road safety, or downtown revitalization—some officials get elected because of a single issue.

Their passion can be helpful, but it also narrows their focus. They may become frustrated when broader policy discussions "waste time" or delay what they care about.

Help them understand the big picture. Show how their issue fits into the city's larger mission and priorities, the city's general plan. Validate their commitment but gently push for balance.

7. They Want to Represent a Specific Group

Diversity in representation is essential—but sometimes, elected officials feel pressure to represent only the narrow interest of the group that got them elected: a neighborhood, a political faction, a religious community.

This can lead to tunnel vision or resistance to compromise.

As a manager, your approach should be bridge-building. Help them understand that while they may advocate for a group, their duty is to govern for all. Support them in becoming more inclusive without denying their core identity.

8. It's a Retirement Hobby or Second Career Move

This is more common than most realize. Someone retires from business, teaching, or law enforcement and wants to stay involved— but on their terms. They bring life experience, but sometimes struggle with structure, process, or transparency.

These electeds can be wonderful resources—or frustrating bottlenecks—depending on how engaged they are and how much they respect staff roles.

Find ways to include them meaningfully. Ask their opinion. Use their experience. But don't let them blur the lines between governing and managing. Be gentle but firm about roles and expectations.

Why It Matters

Understanding why someone ran for office doesn't excuse unacceptable conduct—but it *does* help explain it.

When you know someone's motivation, you can:

- Communicate more effectively.

- Set better boundaries.

- Anticipate conflict.

- Choose your battles wisely.

This doesn't mean you psychoanalyze every elected official. Heavens no! But it *does* mean you remain observant. Listen to what they say. Watch how they vote. Note which issues trigger emotion or frustration. That is their "why." The sooner you understand it the sooner you can adjust your how.

Final Thought: Manage the Person, Not Just the Policy

Your job as a manager isn't just to implement policy. It's to *navigate people*—to understand motivations, manage egos, and align efforts without compromising your ethics.

You are the translator between vision and execution. And that means you need to know not just what your elected officials want—but *why* they want it.

When you learn to lead with curiosity instead of judgment, you'll earn more trust, face fewer surprises, and build stronger working relationships—even with the most difficult personalities.

And this role—this balancing act—doesn't end at policy interpretation. It also, unfortunately, makes you the cheerleader, the referee, the counselor, the mentor, and on some days, the therapist, negotiator, and peacekeeper—sometimes all within the same afternoon. You'll be the person who talks one council member off the ledge while celebrating a victory with another. You'll explain a process for the tenth time, only to be accused of hiding information. You'll stand in the crossfire of interpersonal dynamics that have nothing to do with you—and still be expected to carry the vision forward.

This is not a role for the faint of heart. But it is one of the most vital roles in public service. One that in my opinion has the most impact. And when done with integrity, patience, and an unwavering sense of purpose, it's a role that shapes entire communities.

So manage the people, not just the policy. And above all—lead like you understand the whole chessboard, not just the next move.

◆ Chapter 18 Summary

Understanding why elected officials run for office is essential to managing expectations and leading effectively. Whether driven by ego, activism, anger, or altruism, their motivations shape how they govern—and how you must respond. Your role isn't just to implement policy, but to decode intentions, mediate personalities, and manage agendas without losing your integrity. You are the translator, the referee, the mentor, and sometimes the shield. Know the players. Learn the patterns. Lead with insight—not just instruction.

Chapter 19: National Organizations and Their Role

Understanding the value, limits, and realities of professional associations in the public sector.

In the world of public service, it's easy to assume that professional organizations will be your anchor. Groups like ICMA (International City/County Management Association), GFOA (Government Finance Officers Association), ASPA (American Society for Public Administration), and NFBPA (National Forum for Black Public Administrators) offer training, resources, networking, and sometimes even job boards. They give a sense of professional legitimacy—an institutional backbone that helps define and support your role.

But here's the truth: these organizations are tools—not shields.

Understanding what they offer—and what they don't—is critical if you plan to survive the stormy waters of local government leadership.

What They're Good For

Let's start with the value they do provide, because it is real.

1. Best Practices and Training

Need help developing a policy? Wondering how other cities handled cannabis licensing, homelessness response, or budget deficits? These organizations offer resources that keep you current and thoughtful. Their conferences and webinars help expand your knowledge base and introduce ideas you may not encounter inside your city hall.

2. Peer Networking and Mentorship

One of the greatest benefits of organizations like ICMA is the ability to talk to people who understand what you're going through. You can connect with other managers who've faced the same struggles, survived the same politics, and lived to tell about it. That peer support is vital—especially when you feel isolated in your role.

3. Credentialing and Professional Growth

Whether it's becoming a Credentialed Manager through ICMA or earning specialized certifications through GFOA or the International Management Association (IMA), these credentials enhance your professional standing and signal commitment to ethical leadership.

4. Job Resources and Career Exposure

Some organizations provide resume banks, job postings, and leadership pipelines that can help you move up or over—especially if you're in a smaller jurisdiction trying to break into a larger market. They help you "stay in the game."

5. Thought Leadership and Advocacy for the Profession

Groups like ASPA often publish research on public sector trends, workforce development, and ethics. They help advance the collective thinking about governance and offer a kind of institutional conscience for the field.

What They Will Not Do

And now for the part they don't write in the brochures.

1. They Will Not Defend You When Things Go Bad

If you're being terminated, scapegoated, or politically targeted, don't expect an organization like ICMA or ASPA to come rushing to your aid. Their role is not to litigate your disputes, challenge your dismissal, or publicly question your governing board's actions. They are not unions. They are not legal advocates. They may express disappointment, but they will not stand in the way. And you could not pay enough dues to have them help you through being attacked or fired—that is not their role.

However, it is important to note that most of these organizations do maintain ethical frameworks that allow for anonymous complaints to be submitted against you—sometimes from someone in your own organization, a councilmember, or even a community member. When that happens, they will investigate you. And they will contact your mayor or council. They will call your decision-making, leadership, and professional judgment into question—without revealing who made the complaint, or whether it was politically motivated.

That's the paradox: they won't defend you, but they will investigate you. They won't stand beside you in a public controversy, but they may quietly question your conduct behind the scenes, sometimes without context. While these ethics frameworks are built to uphold professionalism, they can become tools of abuse in the wrong hands—especially in political environments where perception matters more than facts.

So, while they are there to give you best practices and professional development, they won't help you when the rubber hits the road. If you find yourself under attack from elected officials or the public, you'll likely be standing alone.

2. They Won't Save Your Job

These organizations won't confront your mayor or council on your behalf. They won't show up at your special meeting to testify to your leadership. And they certainly won't intervene when someone is trying to paint you as the problem. Their structure isn't designed to advocate for individuals—it's designed to maintain institutional neutrality.

3. They Will Not Challenge Local Politics

They are nonpartisan and neutral by design. That means they will not challenge elected officials, even if those officials are clearly behaving badly, overstepping legal boundaries, or engaging in toxic workplace behavior. If your ethics complaint involves political retaliation or interference, you'll find these groups reluctant to weigh in or take a side.

3. They Might Be More Symbolic Than Supportive

For all their talk of "ethics" and "good governance," these organizations are often much better at offering guidance and language than actual help. When the stakes are high, you don't need a policy brief—you need someone in your corner. Most of these groups can't (and won't) be that person.

4. They Are Not Your Personal Reputation Managers

If you're attacked in the media, wrongly accused, or removed from your position, don't expect them to clear your name. Even if you're completely in the right, they won't risk their own institutional reputation by aligning themselves too closely with any one member. Their goal is to serve the profession—not to protect the individual professional.

So Why Stay Involved?

Despite these few shortcomings, professional organizations still have value—but only if you understand what they actually offer. Think of them like a library, not a lawyer. They provide resources, not rescue. Direction, not defense.

Staying active in these groups helps keep you informed, relevant, and connected. But don't confuse involvement with insulation. Being a dues-paying member or a panel speaker at a national conference won't stop a council from firing you. It won't stop the press from targeting you. It won't stop public opinion from turning on you.

You have to do that work yourself.

That said, you should absolutely stay engaged—but with clear eyes.

Network wisely. Share what you learn. Attend conferences to stay inspired. Seek mentorship. Build relationships with peers who can be your sounding board when things get rough. Just don't mistake the institution for an advocate.

Final Thought: Use the Tools, Don't Worship the Toolbox

These organizations exist to serve the profession—not to save you. They are full of smart, ethical people who want better for local government. I have personally been a dues paying member with several organizations for over 30 years. They provide value, inspiration, and connection. Speaking from personal experience, they will not protect you from political fallout, job loss, or career damage.

So, stay grounded.

Use what's useful. Share what's helpful. And when trouble comes, don't expect the cavalry—be your own cavalry.

Stay professional. Stay ethical. But never outsource your self-awareness or your survival instinct.

And most importantly—don't take anything lying down.

Whether it's your governing board attacking your leadership, or one of these professional organizations opening an investigation against you based on an anonymous complaint, this is where your private documentation, detailed notes, and records become your greatest asset.

Document everything. Protect yourself. And seek legal counsel—not just advice, but real representation. A good attorney will help you understand where you stand, what rights you have, and how to challenge accusations without crossing ethical lines.

If you're under attack, do not capitulate. Do not assume silence will protect you. It won't. Do not assume people will do the right thing. They might not, and normally don't. And do not assume that organizations meant to promote leadership will intervene to protect yours.

They will do what they want to do—especially if you do nothing.

And here's a big reminder of why they often do what they do: while it may be your name on the membership, your city or county is footing the bill. These organizations are aware that the next person in your seat will likely keep the city's dues active. So when you expect them to come to your aid, remember—they're not risking your job. They're protecting a long-term revenue stream. You are temporary. Your agency's check is permanent.

This is the moment your quiet professionalism must become active self-preservation. You've worked too hard, carried too much, and led too many to let it all be erased without a fight.

You don't have to be loud. But you do have to be smart.

Because in this field, the people who survive aren't just the most qualified or the most ethical—they're the ones who stayed alert, stood up, and pushed back when it mattered most.

◆ Chapter 19 Summary

National organizations like ICMA, GFOA, and others can provide valuable resources, best practices, and a sense of community—but they are not your safety net. When the political winds shift or accusations fly, these institutions will not stand between you and fallout. Many have anonymous complaint systems that can question your ethics and leadership without transparency or accountability. And while you may hold the membership, it's your city or county paying the dues—and that's who they're protecting. Use these organizations wisely, but never depend on them to defend your name. In the end, your documentation, your legal strategy, and your integrity are the only true armor you have. Be your own cavalry. Stand your ground. Don't go down quietly. If you are ever challenged by an investigation into your ethics, my recommendation is to call up your attorney as you have more options available to you than you are aware of.

Chapter 20: Support Networks, Ethics Boards, and Advocacy

In the world of public leadership, few things are lonelier than holding the top administrative seat when everything hits the fan. When you're praised, it's shared. When you're criticized, it's personal. And when you're under attack—whether politically, professionally, or personally—the people you thought were in your corner may suddenly become very quiet. This is when support networks matter most. But what most city and county managers eventually learn is this: not all support is supportive, and not all advocacy is advocacy.

This chapter isn't just about where to find support—it's about how to discern *real* support from *performative* support. It's about understanding what ethics boards actually do—and what they won't. It's about preparing for the fact that sometimes, the people and organizations that claim to defend good governance and professional integrity will sit on their hands when you need them most.

This is the reality of advocacy in public administration. It is not what they tell you in orientation.

Support Systems: Who Really Has Your Back?

Everyone tells you to "build your network." That's solid advice. But what they don't tell you is that you don't really *know* your network until you're under pressure. Until you're targeted. Until you're being investigated, politically attacked, or pushed out.

Then you'll learn who returns your calls. Who will write a letter. Who will show up at a council meeting. And—most importantly—who will publicly defend your integrity when the whispers begin.

These people may not be your closest colleagues or most frequent contacts. Sometimes, support comes from people you didn't even know were watching. That quiet assistant city manager in another state. A retired clerk. A staffer you once mentored. These connections matter—and they're built one conversation, one act of kindness, and one shared experience at a time.

Support networks are earned, not inherited. You cultivate them by showing up for others long before you ever need them to show up for you.

Ethics Boards: The Myth and the Mechanism

If you think ethics boards exist to protect you, think again.

Ethics boards—and similar oversight bodies—were created to maintain public trust in institutions, not to defend individual administrators. Their mission is about transparency, not fairness. That distinction matters. Because when you're accused—whether fairly or falsely—they're not there to defend you. They're there to *investigate* you.

Even if the complaint is anonymous. Even if it's baseless. Even if it's politically motivated.

You may never find out who filed the complaint. You may never get a chance to confront the narrative. But you will be scrutinized. And they *will* contact your council, your staff, or even the media in the process of "due diligence."

That's why your personal documentation, your decision-making process, and your professionalism at every stage are critical. You're not just protecting your reputation—you're protecting your livelihood.

The Realities of Advocacy Groups

You might think that professional associations, advocacy nonprofits, or even public good coalitions are there to help you. Some are. Many aren't.

Most have a higher loyalty: to their mission, their brand, and their donor base. If defending you or standing by you compromises their neutrality or their revenue, they'll step back.

It's not personal. It's structural.

These organizations may provide:

- Ethics frameworks and guidelines

- Training materials or workshops

- Best practice templates

- Annual conferences or networking events

But they will rarely step into your defense when you're in political trouble. Why? Because while *you* may be a dues-paying member, your city or county is the one cutting the check. And these groups don't want to jeopardize future access by choosing sides—especially not yours.

You may even find yourself on the receiving end of an ethics "inquiry" or policy investigation prompted by an anonymous complaint, reviewed by one of these very organizations you trusted. It happens more than you think.

What You Can Do Instead

So, what does real support look like in this environment?

1. Build your informal network. Quiet calls with peers. Honest lunches. Behind-the-scenes text threads. These are where the real lifelines exist.

2. Document everything. Don't rely on memory. Don't assume people will remember what happened the way you do. Keep notes, timelines, and receipts.

3. Get a lawyer. When things turn, seek legal counsel. Not your HR director. Not your assistant manager. A professional. And do so early.

4. Don't fight alone. Create a small circle of trusted allies—inside and outside the organization. Their perspective will keep you grounded.

5. Keep showing up. In quiet ways, in consistent ways, let people know you're still present and engaged. That's power.

Final Thought: Stay Alert—You're Experienced

In this profession, advocacy and ethics are more than just ideals—they are your last line of defense when everything else is stripped away. Boards will turn. Allies will vanish. Even organizations you once believed were built to protect public professionals like you may distance themselves when the politics get hot. That's when the real test of your leadership begins.

It's also when your integrity becomes your currency, and you'll be asked—either directly or through pressure—how much it's worth.

I have been sued professionally and personally as a city manager for $100 million. I did not lose that lawsuit or any other lawsuit for a municipality. I've settled every single lawsuit brought against my organizations that happened prior to my arrival. But none of that means anything when someone decides they want you gone. Not facts. Not history. Not performance. When the campaign starts, they'll say you're absent, that you don't communicate well, that you've defied council direction, or that you're unethical. They will say or do anything to create the narrative that suits their purpose.

I've had to leave organizations where the message was clear: stay and break the law—or go quietly. I've been asked to sweep things under the rug, ignore internal wrongdoing, or simply not report violations I uncovered. In each case, the moral burden fell squarely on me—

because as the city manager, everything is your responsibility, even if it's not your fault.

And when they let you go, it won't matter how much you gave, how many awards you won, or how many buildings stand because of your work. The only thing that will matter is how you protected your credibility when it counted.

So, here's what I've learned:

- Document everything. Don't take anything lying down. Don't let fear or fatigue keep you from standing up for the truth.

- Get a good attorney. Not when you're in trouble—before you're in trouble. Know your rights, your contracts, and your protections.

- Don't do it alone. If you're going to take a stand, make sure it's not a solo act. Find allies, mentors, even advocacy organizations—but walk into the storm prepared.

- Know when your legacy is at stake. And remember: Your name is not for sale.

Public leadership is a lonely place. But you were not built for comfort—you were built for purpose. And when the political winds shift, when your back is against the wall, when they say "just stay quiet and we'll forget it happened"—you have a choice.

You can stay silent and stay safe.

Or you can lead.

But don't let them break you. Not over a job. Not over a paycheck. Not over pressure.

Because at the end of it all, when the headlines fade and the council or board has moved on, your integrity is all that remains.

And it's either the shield that protected you—or the evidence that convicts you.

◆ **Chapter 20 Summary**

In public leadership, support is not guaranteed—even from the organizations and individuals who claim to stand beside you. Ethics boards, professional associations, and advocacy groups often prioritize neutrality or politics over your defense. This chapter reveals the hard truths of advocacy and the importance of documenting your integrity, building informal support networks, and preparing for betrayal. When the attacks come—and they will—your preparation, your allies, and your principles will be all that stand between your career and collapse. Integrity isn't just a virtue—it's your armor, your currency, and your legacy.

Chapter 21: Know When It's Time to Walk Away

There comes a moment in every public leader's career—no matter how resilient, passionate, or experienced—when the question arises: *Is it time to go?* Not out of failure. Not because you've lost your fight. But because staying any longer could cost you more than you're willing to pay.

Walking away isn't quitting. In fact, it may be the most courageous act of leadership you ever perform. It requires the kind of self-awareness, humility, and wisdom that many leaders never develop until it's too late.

This chapter is about recognizing that moment. The signs. The feelings. The internal negotiations you make when your passion is at odds with your peace of mind. And the practical and emotional strategies needed to leave with your health, your dignity, and your legacy intact.

The Warning Signs Aren't Always Loud

You likely won't wake up one day and suddenly know it's time. It starts as something smaller.

- You dread meetings—not because of the content, but the people.

- You feel exhausted not from the hours, but from the politics.

- You've started to rationalize ethical gray areas because pushing back seems futile.

- Your once-sharp instincts are now dulled by second-guessing and burnout.

- Your family is telling you you've changed—and not for the better.

These are early indicators. They aren't weaknesses. They're signals. And great leaders pay attention to signals.

There's no shame in fatigue. But there's danger in ignoring it.

What Are You Staying For?

Before you make any decision, ask yourself one clarifying question: *What or why am I staying for?*

If the answer is purpose, people, or unfinished work—there may still be a fight worth fighting.

But if the answer is fear, pride, a pension, or simply habit, then you owe it to yourself to reflect more deeply.

Your "why" matters. Because staying without one not only hurts you—it harms the organization. A disengaged leader creates a leadership vacuum. And vacuums get filled—often by chaos, resentment, or opportunism.

Legacy Over Loyalty

Too many city and county managers stay too long because they mistake loyalty to their organization with loyalty to their position.

You can still love the work and serve the community by stepping aside. In fact, sometimes it's the most selfless thing you can do, especially when your continued presence becomes a distraction, a lightning rod, or an excuse for dysfunction.

Your legacy isn't how long you stayed. It's *how you left.*

Did you prepare your team for your absence?

Did you protect the institution rather than defend your ego?

Did you model grace, maturity, and accountability?

Your Health Is the Red Line

You cannot serve if you're broken. And public service will break you if you let it.

When your stress turns into chronic physical symptoms, when anxiety keeps you up at night, when you're distant from your family, when your mind is elsewhere even on weekends, it's time to re-evaluate.

There's a point where staying becomes a health hazard. And no city council, no policy initiative, no legacy is worthy of your body or mind.

Take the vacation. Use the sick time. But most importantly, know when the time off won't fix it—and when the only real healing comes from stepping away.

Making the Exit: How to Walk Away with Grace

If you decide the time has come, here's how to do it right:

1. **Control Your Narrative:** Don't let others write your exit story. Be clear, firm, and positive in your messaging.

2. **Protect Your Team:** Don't scapegoat. Don't blame. Leave in a way that allows them to keep doing good work.

3. **Tie Off Loose Ends:** Close out major projects, prepare transition memos, and offer to help onboard your successor.

4. **Communicate with the Community:** They may not all like you, but they deserve closure.

5. **Exit with Dignity:** Don't burn bridges—even the ones that burned you. Your integrity is yours to carry forward.

Final Thought: Knowing When Enough Is Enough

There is no honor in sacrificing yourself for a system that will keep churning and moving without you.

You were never meant to stay forever. You were meant to lead for a season, to build something better, and to pass the baton.

Knowing when to fight is leadership.

Knowing when to walk away is wisdom.

And doing so with your head held high is legacy.

When you say goodbye, give yourself space—physically, emotionally, and professionally. Step back from the profession, even if just for a few months. That time away is not a retreat—it's a reset. You need distance to see clearly. You need silence to hear your own thoughts again.

Use that time not only to process what just happened but to prepare—strategically, emotionally, and, if needed, legally. If there are issues that require response or accountability, be thoughtful and deliberate. Let your next steps be rooted in clarity, not reaction.

But most importantly, use this pause to rediscover your purpose. Evaluate your journey. Reflect on what you've learned—not just about others, but about yourself. Ask the hard questions: What parts of me did I give away? What am I no longer willing to sacrifice? What makes me excited to lead again?

Because the point is not to walk away broken. The point is to walk away intact—and stronger.

And remember this isn't just about a job, it's about your life. Your health. Your spirit. Your dignity. And most of all—your integrity.

If you can still look in the mirror and be proud of the person staring back at you, then you've done something right. No title or paycheck is worth more than that quiet confidence in your character.

I remember when my kids were young, we'd sit across the dinner table at night and each take turns sharing the "good" and "bad" of our day. It became a simple, grounding ritual. But over time, I started measuring my actions against it. I decided: *If I couldn't tell my kids what I did that day, I probably shouldn't have done it at all.*

That became my inner compass. And it can be yours too.

So, when the end comes—whether you chose it or it chose you—let it come on your terms. With clarity. With pride. With the peace that you led the right way, even when it cost you.

Don't let politics rob you of joy. Don't let bitterness replace your belief in public service. Don't let betrayal steal your identity.

Get your motivation back. Find your smile again.

Because you are more than the title. And if you honor the person in the mirror, your legacy will speak for itself.

◆ **Chapter 21 Summary**

Walking away is not failure, it's wisdom. True leadership knows when to stay and when to leave. Your job is not your identity, and your legacy is not defined by your title but by your integrity. When it's time to go, step away with clarity, protect your health and spirit, and reclaim your purpose. Let the mirror—not the headlines—be your measure. And never forget, you are more than the role you once held.

Chapter 22: The End of the Road

There comes a moment in every public servant's journey where the road begins to narrow. The victories may feel fewer. The criticisms louder. The excitement for "what's next" gives way to a quiet question: *Have I done enough?*

Whether you're forced out, choose to leave, or find yourself somewhere in between, the end of a public career is rarely clean. It's layered, emotional, and deeply personal. You've likely given years— maybe decades—of your life to the service of others. You've stood in the storm, taken the heat, defended your team, and pushed through decisions no one else wanted to touch.

And now, it's time to walk away.

But how do you do that when the job has become part of your identity? When your name has been on every press release, every resolution, every capital improvement plan? When you've sacrificed family dinners, vacations, and sleep—all for a role that can end with one closed-session vote?

This chapter is about the emotional, mental, and practical realities of ending a career in public leadership. Whether you walk out the front door on your own terms or through the back door under pressure, the exit matters. Because how you leave says just as much as how you led.

Facing the Final Chapter with Clarity

Leaving doesn't always come with applause. Sometimes, it's silence. Sometimes, it's relief—from others, not you. Sometimes, it's messy, fast, and undeserved.

You may not get a party, a plaque, or a handshake. You may get escorted out.

Or maybe you leave with dignity and grace, but deep inside, you're grieving. That's normal. You're not just leaving a job, you're closing a chapter of service, commitment, and identity.

Give yourself permission to feel it all. There's no weakness in mourning something you gave so much to. It means you cared.

But don't stay in that place. Grieve it. Then begin again.

You Were Not the Title

The hardest adjustment is realizing the emails will stop. The phone won't ring as much. The decisions will be made without you.

When your nameplate comes off the door, you'll confront a deeper truth: *Who am I without this job?*

And here's your answer—you are still someone of value.

You are the sum of your leadership, your integrity, your relationships, and your lessons. You are not your title. You are not your final paycheck. And you are certainly not the opinion of the last council that let you go.

Let the role go, not your worth.

Final Thought: Exit Like a Leader, Not a Victim

There is no perfect goodbye. But there is a powerful one.

When you say goodbye, take time away from the profession—and from your last job. If that's a few months, great. If it's more, even better. Take time to think, to reflect, and not only prepare to act on what just occurred—legally, emotionally, and professionally—but to heal.

This is about your *life*, your *health*, your *spirit*, your *dignity*, and—above all—your *integrity*.

You may feel broken, but that's temporary. I have fought wars for cities and taken beatings—often and accordingly—especially for doing the right thing for myself, for staff, and for the community. I've watched elected officials say they're always right—even when there are five, seven, or ten of them disagreeing with each other.

Whether you carry forward in this career or walk away from it, just know it may take time to find the next job or career path. It will be easy to feel defeated. That's when you need your support systems. Lean on them. Let them carry you until you find your footing again.

Remember, as long as you can look in the mirror and be okay with the person staring back—that's what matters most.

I remember when I was younger, I thought that it was easy to distinguish between, "good" and "bad", but just like talking with my boys, things get more difficult and not easily explained. Sometimes, the difference between the two, isn't legal, policy written, or a directive – but more of a staple to how we were brought up to determine the difference. If we stick to how we see good and bad as a child, it would make our jobs and working with others so much easier.

This profession will push you, break you, challenge you, and change you. But it will also strengthen you, shape you, and teach you resilience in ways few careers can.

You are not alone.

You are not a failure.

You are not forgotten.

You are someone who stood up—again and again—when it mattered most.

And now, it's time to stand up for yourself.

Leaving public service isn't just a career transition—it's an emotional reckoning. Whether you walk out with applause or accusations, your exit matters. Be intentional, take the time to reflect, heal, and reclaim your identity beyond the title. This is about your integrity, your health, and your legacy. The end of one road may be the beginning of another—one you get to choose on your own terms.

Chapter 23: The Media Friend, Foe, or Force of Nature?

There is no escaping the media. Whether it's the local newspaper, a regional television station, or a citizen journalist armed with nothing more than a cell phone and a social media account, every city manager learns quickly that the press is a constant companion. Sometimes it will work to your advantage. Sometimes it will seem like the most formidable adversary you face. And often, it is simply a force of nature—indifferent, relentless, and powerful—shaping the perception of your leadership and your organization.

The Press Is Not Your Friend

This is the first truth you must accept: the press is not your friend. Reporters may be friendly. They may call you often. They may laugh with you before or after an interview. But do not mistake cordiality for loyalty. A reporter's allegiance is not to you, your staff, or your community, it is to the story.

And if the best story happens to cast you or your organization in a negative light, they will not hesitate to write it. That doesn't make them villains; it makes them professionals doing their job. But it does mean you must approach every interaction with clarity about your role. You are not in a friendship. You are in a transactional relationship.

This can be difficult for managers who value connection and trust. In our profession, we thrive on building coalitions, nurturing staff, and fostering partnerships. The media tempts us to extend that same trust to reporters. Resist it. Respect them, yes. Be professional, yes. But never let your guard down.

A reporter who calls you for "background" is still a reporter doing their job. They may present themselves as allies in uncovering the truth, but their priority is not your protection—it is their byline.

Nothing Is Ever Off the Record

There is perhaps no more dangerous phrase in public administration than "off the record." It lures you in with a false sense of safety, as if the words you are about to speak will vanish into a vault. The truth? If it helps their story, if it adds drama, or if it gives them leverage, your words may still find their way to print.

Even if the reporter themselves honors the agreement, there is no guarantee that an editor won't push for inclusion or that the context won't leak in another form. And once it leaks, the trail will lead back to you.

I once watched a colleague fall into this trap. Believing he was off the record, he made a sarcastic comment about a council member's ego. Days later, a columnist—who hadn't even been present—referenced "insider frustrations with the mayor's personality." The dots were easy to connect. The damage to his relationship with the council was immediate and lasting.

The rule is simple: if you would not want your words printed in tomorrow's paper or plastered across a headline, do not say them— ever. Assume every microphone is live, every camera is rolling, and every conversation can become public. This mindset may feel cautious, even paranoid. But it will save your career.

The Double-Edged Sword of Exposure

At its best, the media can elevate the work of your staff, highlight the progress your community is making, and create positive narratives that help build trust with residents. A feature story on a new park, a spotlight on your first responders, or even an editorial praising fiscal responsibility can remind the public that government is functioning as it should.

But exposure is not always positive. One angry resident's comment can become a headline. A personnel issue you're legally barred from discussing may become front-page news. And the timing is rarely under your control.

The reality is that media operates on deadlines, not governance timelines. The news cycle does not pause for your council meeting schedule, nor does it wait for you to gather all the facts. The mismatch of pace—media's urgency versus government's deliberation—creates friction. The public often assumes silence means guilt or evasion. But as a manager, you may be constrained by confidentiality, contracts, or ongoing investigations. That silence, however necessary, leaves a vacuum that the media is all too willing to fill.

Once It's Out There, It Lives Forever

There is one rule about public perception that should be etched into every manager's mind: once something is in print, online, or in a picture, it takes on a life of its own—and it never goes away.

A misquote in a small-town paper can resurface years later when you apply for another position. A photograph taken at an awkward moment can be weaponized out of context. A single statement, even if clarified later, can define you more than years of dedicated service.

I recall a time I worked for a municipality; I was at City Hall on live television welcoming people to downtown – in that moment I said "Welcome to Town Hell". I was so shocked that it came out of my mouth and on live TV! However, most of the time we have to self-correct, own the moment, and move on. Understand that direct and honest communication will always help after a difficult moment.

In the digital age, nothing disappears. Even deleted articles linger in archives. Screenshots preserve tweets long after they are erased. And videos—once posted—become permanent records shared endlessly across platforms.

I once had to counsel a colleague who was photographed at a community festival holding a beer. Innocent enough. But the picture, taken by a resident, was shared on social media with the caption "City manager drinking on the job." The narrative snowballed. No explanation about it being a Saturday off-duty event could undo the initial impression.

That is the reality: perception outruns truth. And perception, once shaped, rarely changes. Every word, every action, every setting must be considered through the lens of permanence. Before you speak, ask yourself: *If this quote were on the front page tomorrow, would I stand by it?* Before you act, ask: *If this picture circulated online forever, what would it say about me?*

Relationships Matter More Than Sound Bites

Despite these dangers, relationships still matter. Reporters who know you to be honest, responsive, and professional are more likely to present your side fairly. They may still write hard stories, but the tone and framing can soften when they respect you.

A practical rule I followed was this: treat every interaction with the media as if it were on the record. Even when a journalist says otherwise, remain disciplined. The safest way to build trust without risk is to be consistent, factual, and restrained.

At the same time, do not fall into the trap of overexposure. If you become the face of every issue, you will also be the face of every controversy. Step forward when it is your responsibility, particularly in crises. Step back and let staff or elected officials take the spotlight when appropriate.

Crisis Communication: The Test of Leadership

No test of leadership with the media is greater than a crisis. Whether it is a natural disaster, a financial scandal, or a tragic event in the community, the media will descend immediately.

In those moments, three principles matter most:

1. **Acknowledge reality quickly.** Silence breeds mistrust. Even a simple, "We are aware of the situation, and our first priority is safety," is better than no response.

2. **Provide facts, not speculation.** Stick to what you know and promise updates as more information becomes available.

3. **Show empathy.** Communities want to see that their leaders care, not just that they can recite data.

Tone is everything. Calm, steady words in a crisis may be remembered longer than the crisis itself.

The Rise of Social Media

If traditional media is a double-edged sword, social media is a chainsaw—powerful, useful, but dangerous in unskilled hands. Today, every resident with a smartphone can broadcast live from a council meeting. Every policy can be debated, misquoted, and distorted in real time.

The temptation for many managers is to ignore social media. Don't. While you should not argue with every critic, you cannot abandon the space. Cities must provide accurate, consistent updates through official channels. Otherwise, misinformation fills the gap.

Equally important is training your staff. A careless tweet from an employee can cause chaos. Establish policies, set expectations, and model professionalism.

◆ Chapter 23 Summary

The media is not your ally, nor is it always your adversary—it is a force to be managed with discipline. Never forget: the press is not your friend, nothing is ever truly off the record, and once something is public, it lives forever. Your words and actions must be chosen with the knowledge that perception often outlasts fact. In leadership, survival depends not only on what you do but on how the story is told.

Chapter 24: Family, Health, and the Human Side of Leadership

Public service is a calling. It demands long hours, endless meetings, constant preparation, and a willingness to absorb pressure that others cannot or will not bear. But behind every city manager—the long council agendas, the budget battles, the political storms—stands a human being. And behind that human being often stands a family, or friends, or loved ones who feel the ripple effects of every late-night meeting and every public controversy.

Too often, in our drive to serve the community, we neglect the cost of this profession on our own well-being and on those closest to us. The truth is simple: you cannot lead effectively for the long term if you sacrifice your health, your family, or your humanity along the way.

The Hidden Toll on Families

When you take the chair as city manager, your family does not just gain a title by association, they inherit the scrutiny that comes with it. Spouses become recognizable at the grocery store. Children hear whispers at school. A single critical article in the newspaper may find its way into dinner conversations you never imagined.

I know this toll firsthand. As a father, I began to see all the moments I was missing with my kids. Games, dinners, conversations that should have been ordinary parts of family life became sacrifices to the calendar of council meetings, community events, and crises. At the time, I justified it as part of the job. But over time, the imbalance grew so great that it cost me my marriage.

The irony is that once the marriage ended, I was given full custody of my boys. Suddenly, everything shifted. I could no longer pretend that being work-centered above all else was sustainable. I had to refocus—

not just for myself, but because I was the foundation of stability for them. The lesson is stark: you can lose everything at home if you allow the job to consume you. The community will replace you in a heartbeat. Your family cannot.

Keeping Family Separate from Public Service

One of the firm lines I have held throughout my career is this: I never actively or consistently involved my kids or my family in my public sector work. Some managers do, bringing their families to ribbon cuttings, parades, or press events. That is their choice, but I found it dangerous for several reasons.

First, it blurs boundaries. When your family becomes a part of your public role, their identity becomes tied to your job. If residents dislike you, your family will feel that dislike as well. Second, family dynamics—normally private—can suddenly find their way into the press. Arguments, divorces, or even simple personal details can be exposed or weaponized. Third, familiarity is a double-edged sword. When people know your spouse or children by name and face, they sometimes forget where the professional boundary should lie. Just remember while you may acknowledge others and their families, and know your boundaries, others may not.

The safest course is to protect your family's privacy. Your kids deserve the right to be kids, not the "city manager's kids." Your spouse deserves to be recognized for who they are, not as an extension of your office. Keeping that separation helps protect them from the unavoidable turbulence of public life.

Health: The Silent Casualty

The second toll of leadership is personal health. Managers are not immune to stress—we are often drowning in it. Every decision seems high stakes. Every crisis demands attention. And every moment of rest feels stolen.

Stress has a way of settling into the body. Poor diet from late-night fast food after meetings. Lack of exercise because the schedule is always too tight. Sleepless nights replaying council debates or preparing for tomorrow's battles. Slowly, without noticing, you trade your physical health and wellbeing for professional endurance.

For me, the wake-up call was not theoretical. I let my health go—and it nearly killed me. I became very sick, terminally sick, because I put the job above my own body. The hours, the commitments, the unrelenting pressure created a slow erosion that I didn't fully recognize until it was too late.

That forced me to restructure and reset my life. No title, no contract, no praise from a council chamber is worth your life. If you lose your health, you lose everything—the job, the family, the chance to continue serving.

This is a thankless job at times. It can be rewarding, but the costs are high. If you take nothing else from my experience, remember this: whether emotionally, physically, or professionally, you must always protect yourself. I think this is one of the greatest jobs in the world, but remember there are risks in any job.

Emotional Resilience and Burnout

Physical health is only half the battle. Emotional resilience—the ability to weather criticism, betrayal, and constant pressure—is what sustains you through the storms. But emotional reserves are finite.

Every angry email from a resident, every council member who questions your integrity, every rumor about your leadership—these things add up. They don't simply vanish after the meeting adjourns. They stay with you, sometimes long into the night.

Burnout creeps in quietly. You begin to feel detached, going through the motions. The passion that once drove you to serve fades under the weight of cynicism. Some managers quit abruptly when burnout overtakes them. Others stay but become shells of their former selves, coasting until retirement.

To survive, you must recognize the signs early: fatigue that doesn't lift, irritability with family, dread of the next council meeting. And you must find ways to replenish—through hobbies, friendships outside of work, professional counseling, or simple time away.

The Importance of Boundaries

Boundaries are perhaps the hardest lesson for a city manager to learn. In a profession built on accessibility and accountability, saying "no" feels unnatural, even selfish. But boundaries are not selfish, it's how you survive. .

Boundaries mean not answering calls at 2 a.m. unless it's a true emergency. Boundaries mean protecting family vacations without constant interruption. Boundaries mean telling yourself—and others—that your health is not negotiable.

When you fail to set boundaries, you send a signal: your time and well-being are secondary to the whims of politics and crisis. When you set them, you model healthy leadership and give your staff permission to do the same.

Rediscovering Humanity in Leadership

At its core, leadership is not about endless stamina, it is about being human while managing an inhuman load. It is about showing staff that you too need rest, that resilience comes from balance, and that strength includes vulnerability.

I have often said: *You cannot be a good manager if you are not a good person at first.* Being a good person means being present for your family, caring for your health, and acknowledging your limits. A community may ask for superhuman leadership, but what it truly needs is steady, compassionate, human leadership.

◆ **Chapter 24 Summary**

The community may demand all of you, but it does not deserve the sacrifice of your family or your health. Leadership is thankless at times, rewarding at others—but always dangerous if you forget to protect yourself. I lost a marriage, nearly lost my health, and was forced to refocus my life because of this profession. Learn from that: set boundaries, guard your family's privacy, and never let the work consume so much of you that there is nothing left to give. The job is temporary. Your life is not.

Chapter 25: The Paper Trail: Protect Yourself

In different parts of this book, I have mentioned the importance of documentation—sometimes in passing, sometimes as part of a larger point about survival in public service. However, I felt this subject was so critical that it deserved its own chapter. If you take nothing else from this manuscript, take this: *document everything.*

Politics is fickle. Councils change. Memories fade. Narratives shift. But documents—emails, memos, meeting notes, reports—create a paper trail that can save your career, protect your reputation, and, in some cases, keep you out of legal jeopardy.

Documentation is not paranoia. It is survival.

Why Documentation Matters

Every city manager learns quickly that decisions rarely exist in a vacuum. A directive given in confidence today can be denied tomorrow. A request from an elected official can later be reframed as your "overreach." A conversation about priorities can suddenly be forgotten when political winds shift.

When that happens, your best protection is not what you remember, it's what you can prove.

Councils and attorneys alike will ask: *What do the records show?* If your answer is nothing but recollection, you are vulnerable. If your answer is a memo, an email, or a written directive, you are protected.

I have sat in more than one closed session where elected officials claimed they had never approved or discussed a particular initiative. Without documentation, it would have been my word against theirs. With documentation, the record spoke for itself.

The Discipline of Follow-Up

One of the most practical tools you can use is the follow-up email. After a meeting or conversation where direction is given, send a professional, factual recap. It doesn't need to be long. A simple:

> "To confirm our discussion, the council directed staff to move forward with XYZ. Please let me know if this understanding is not accurate."

That one paragraph creates a record. It clarifies expectations. It closes the door to revisionist history later.

The same is true after conversations with mayors or individual council members. A quick memo to the file, or a brief note to yourself with date, time, and topic, can later prove invaluable.

The Courtroom Test

Always remember this: anything you document may one day end up in court.

That doesn't mean you shouldn't write—it means you must write with discipline. Keep documentation factual, professional, and free of emotion. Don't editorialize. Don't vent in writing. Don't assume a text message is private.

If you stick to facts—what was said, what was directed, what action was taken—your documentation will serve you well. If you let anger or frustration bleed into the record, it may one day be used against you.

The Importance of Paper Copies

In today's digital age, it may seem like everything can live in your email or your hard drive. But digital records are vulnerable. Emails can be deleted by IT policies, hacked, or even accessed by those looking to discredit you.

That's why it is especially important to always keep paper copies of your notes. A paper record cannot be altered without leaving evidence. It cannot disappear with the push of a button, and only destroyed out of your possession.

But there's another critical rule: never keep those records in your office. Your office belongs to the city, not to you. When you are terminated or asked to leave, you will be locked out with no opportunity to retrieve files. Everything inside becomes city property. The primary concern here is that every city, county and states have their own retention rules, and may delete everything after 60 days, etc.

The safe practice is to always do your daily recap at home, not at city hall. Keep your personal notes, memos, and recaps securely in your home office or another safe place under your control.

And this is just as important: How you conduct yourselves is your personal business. This is your safety net. The fewer people who know about it, the safer it is. If asked, you are simply being professional with emails, staff reports, and council packets. Your personal records remain private.

Protecting Yourself from Scapegoating

One of the unfortunate realities of city management is that when something goes wrong, someone must take the blame. More often than not, that someone is the city manager.

Documentation is your shield against scapegoating. If a directive was given by the council, and you carried it out, your record should reflect that. If a policy decision was made at the political level, your notes should make that clear.

This doesn't guarantee you won't be blamed—but it ensures you have the evidence to defend your actions, whether in the press, in a closed session, or in a courtroom.

The Role of Memos to File

Not every directive is given publicly. Sometimes a mayor or council member pulls you aside after a meeting and says, "Don't put this in writing, but here's what I want."

That's exactly when you should document it.

A "memo to file"—dated, factual, stored securely—is your record of what occurred. If that request later comes into question, you have a contemporaneous account. Without it, the request can be denied, and you are left exposed.

Technology, Transparency, and Permanence

In today's world, documentation is not just about paper. Emails, texts, and digital files often become public records. That means you must assume that anything you write can and will be read by others someday.

This reality cuts both ways:

- It forces discipline in tone and content.

- It ensures transparency protects you as much as it constrains you.

When a request under the Freedom of Information Act or a state public records law comes in, you want to feel confident—not fearful—about what will be revealed.

Documenting for Yourself

Documentation is not only about protecting yourself from others—it's also about protecting yourself from yourself.

In the rush of endless meetings, it's easy to forget details. Notes help you track commitments, recall timelines, and prepare for questions months later.

I once had a council member challenge me on a statement I allegedly made nearly a year prior. Thanks to my notes, I was able to provide the exact date, context, and language. Without that record, I would have been defenseless.

The Discipline That Saves Careers

Over the years, I have known managers who lost their jobs not because of performance, but because they had no documentation to prove the truth. I have also known managers who survived attacks precisely because they could produce a clear paper trail.

The difference is discipline. Documenting everything takes time, patience, and consistency. But in the long run, it is one of the best investments you can make in your career.

Documentation is protection. Keep daily recaps in paper form. Whether through follow-up emails, memos, or personal notes, a clear paper trail can shield you from scapegoating, clarify directives, and preserve the truth long after memories fade. In public service, your word is not enough. Records matter. The paper trail is the difference between vulnerability and survival.

Chapter 26: Reinventing yourself after Public Service

Every city manager eventually reaches a crossroads. Sometimes it comes when a contract ends abruptly. Sometimes it comes after years of steady service when burnout sets in. Other times it comes by choice, when you decide it's time for a new chapter.

The truth is that careers in public service rarely end neatly. Unlike the private sector, where retirement parties and planned transitions are common, public administrators often leave suddenly, pushed out by politics, worn down by the pace, or forced by circumstances beyond their control. When that day arrives, the question becomes: *What now?*

Reinvention is not optional. It is survival.

Whether You Leave in Shambles or at the Peak

One of the hardest truths about this profession is that you don't always get to choose how you leave. Some managers walk away at the peak of success—applauded by staff, appreciated by the community, remembered for transformational projects. Others are forced out in controversy, caught in political crossfire, or blamed for problems that began long before they arrived.

Whether you left your last job in shambles or at the peak of success, the question remains: what's next? And here's the key— *how you leave will dictate how you reinvent yourself later.*

If you leave on good terms, you can leverage positive references, carry a reputation for stability, and transition smoothly into consulting, teaching, or other roles. If you leave under fire, your reinvention may take longer. You may need to repair credibility, explain circumstances carefully, and prove yourself in a new context.

Neither path is impossible. Both require reflection, humility, and strategy. What matters most is that you don't let the circumstances of your departure permanently define you. You can—and must—write the next chapter.

When the End Comes Suddenly

There's another truth that many city managers don't want to hear: when your career path comes to an end, sometimes it's not by your choice—and it will happen fast.

I've seen managers go from celebrated to unemployed in a matter of hours, often after nothing more than a single council vote or a closed-session decision. There are no guarantees in this profession. You may not see it coming, and yet, in an instant, everything changes.

That's why you must always be prepared, even when you don't see that day coming tomorrow. Keep your résumé updated. Keep your network active. Keep your financial reserves healthy. Waiting until the day you're pushed out to start thinking about your next step is too late.

Preparation doesn't mean you're disloyal to your current city. It means you're realistic about the volatility of this profession. A council can love you today and cut ties tomorrow. Be proud of your service, but never let the illusion of permanence blind you to the possibility of sudden change.

Reinvention Takes Time

Too many managers believe reinvention should be immediate—that the day after a contract ends, they must have a new job lined up. The reality is different. Reinvention takes time. You have to heal, regroup, and rediscover who you are outside the role.

The most dangerous mistake is to sit idle, letting resentment or bitterness fester. Keep busy. Take on small consulting projects, volunteer, write, mentor, or explore new learning opportunities. Activity keeps your mind engaged and your confidence intact while you sort out your next direction.

I often recommend to colleagues: if you can afford it, take a breather—a break for a year. Reset your health, reconnect with your family, and allow yourself the space to think about what you truly want. A pause is not failure; it is preparation. Some of my clearest career decisions came not in the middle of council chambers but in the quiet months between roles.

Start With What You Know Best—You

When you are ready to move forward, begin with what you know best: **yourself.** Reinvention is not about becoming someone you are not. It is about reframing and redirecting the expertise you already have.

Ask yourself: What skills came most naturally to me as a manager? Was it fiscal discipline? Crisis leadership? Personnel management? Strategic planning? Those strengths form the foundation of your next chapter.

Your expertise and knowledge base. Translate city hall language into broader terms that apply elsewhere. Instead of saying, "I managed council priorities," you can say, "I aligned competing stakeholder interests." Instead of "I balanced a city budget," you can say, "I oversaw multimillion-dollar financial operations." These subtle shifts reposition your experience for consulting firms, universities, nonprofits, or the private sector.

The Role of Trusted Friends and Advisors

Reinvention is not a solo project. It requires perspective—and sometimes we are the least objective about ourselves when we're in transition. This is where close friends and trusted advisors come in.

Work with those who know you best. Seek their guidance. Friends outside the profession can see strengths you take for granted. Mentors can help you frame your experience in ways that resonate with different audiences. Sometimes, a simple conversation with someone who cares about you as a person, not just as a professional, can unlock the clarity you need.

When I left a role under pressure, it was a friend—not a recruiter, not a professional coach—who reminded me that my value wasn't tied to a single city council's opinion. That encouragement helped me take the first step toward rebuilding. Don't underestimate the power of your circle.

The Portable Skills of Leadership

Years of balancing budgets, managing staff, navigating crises, and negotiating with elected officials create skills that translate across industries.

- **Crisis management** applies in nonprofits, corporations, and education.

- **Fiscal responsibility** is prized in the private sector as much as in government.

- **Personnel leadership** is a universal skill.

- **Political navigation**—while unique in the public arena—sharpens strategic thinking that can be invaluable in consulting or advocacy roles.

The trick is learning to frame your experience in new language and demonstrating that your leadership has value beyond city hall.

Paths After Public Service

Reinvention looks different for everyone. Some common paths include:

- **Consulting** — Offering guidance to cities, nonprofits, or private firms looking to navigate government relations.

- **Teaching and Academia** — Sharing lessons with the next generation of public servants.

- **Private Sector Leadership** — Bringing discipline and management to corporations or startups.

- **Nonprofit or Advocacy Work** — Serving missions with more freedom and focus.

- **Elected Office** — For those who want to bring administrative experience into policymaking.

Identity Beyond the Title

Perhaps the hardest shift is letting go of the title. For years, "city manager" may have defined who you are. Losing that role can feel like losing your identity. But you are more than the title.

You are a leader, a strategist, a mentor, a parent, a friend. Reinvention requires rediscovering that person again. The role ends. You do not.

Preparing Before the End Comes

The best reinventions start before the end arrives. Build networks outside of city hall. Keep your résumé sharp. Save financially so you have flexibility. Continue developing skills that apply across industries. These steps are not disloyal—they are wise.

Because if there's one certainty in this line of work, it's that the end may come fast—and when it does, only those who prepared will land on their feet.

Resentment or Renewal

When careers end abruptly, resentment is natural. But carrying bitterness only poisons you. Renewal, on the other hand, gives you power. Choosing renewal means deciding that the next chapter is not defined by the last. It means owning your scars, but not being defined by them.

The Gift of Perspective

In hindsight, reinvention can become one of the greatest gifts of a public service career. It forces you to reassess priorities, opens doors you never considered, and reminds you that your worth does not depend on a council vote.

For me, reinvention meant rediscovering my health, reconnecting with my family, and finding ways to use my experience beyond the walls of city hall. It meant understanding that while the profession can be thankless at times, it does not define the sum of your life.

Every public service career will eventually end—and sometimes it happens suddenly, without warning, and not by your choice. How you leave will shape how you reinvent yourself, so always be prepared. Take time to reset, keep yourself busy, lean on trusted friends, and start with what you know best: you. Reinvention takes patience and perspective, but it transforms endings into beginnings. The job can end in an instant. Your ability to adapt, thrive, and lead does not.

Epilogue: After the Title Is Gone

The city manager's office eventually gets a new occupant. The business cards change. The email address is reassigned. Your picture and the website is removed and a new person's face is there. The decisions you made—whether celebrated or scrutinized—become part of the city's ongoing story. But leadership isn't measured by plaques on the wall or proclamations handed out at your farewell reception. It's measured in the moments no one saw, the battles you chose not to fight publicly, and the people who grew stronger under your leadership.

When the meetings are over and your inbox finally stops filling, what remains is the impact you had on people—your staff, your community, and even your critics. It's not about whether you stayed until retirement. It's about whether you stayed true to yourself.

Public service is never just a job. It's a calling—one that demands your time, your energy, your patience, and too often, your peace. But it also shapes you in ways few professions can. It teaches resilience. It deepens empathy. It tests your values and reveals your true self under pressure.

You will leave the profession changed. Hopefully wiser. Maybe scarred. But if you led with courage, transparency, and integrity—then you led well.

Let that be your legacy. Not the office you held, but the way you held yourself while in it.

Because long after the headlines fade and the titles are gone, your integrity remains. And in this work—that's everything.

Final Thoughts: The Quiet Strength of Leadership

Leadership in public service isn't about titles, contracts, or the moments when the cameras are rolling. It's about what happens when the cameras are gone — when the council meeting ends, the lights dim, and you're left alone with the weight of decisions that few will ever understand.

What this journey has shown, time and again, is that true leadership is not about being right; it's about being steady. It's about showing up when it would be easier to walk away, and doing the ethical thing when no one is watching — especially when doing the right thing costs you something personally.

Every city manager, department head, or public administrator who reads this knows what that means. You've felt the crossfire between politics and principle. You've watched integrity tested by convenience. You've endured moments when silence was safer than truth. And yet, you pressed forward — because the work mattered, and the people mattered more.

If there's one takeaway from all of this, it's that leadership in government is not defined by how long you last, but by how you leave. Your reputation is the echo of every decision you made under pressure, every staff member you defended when it was unpopular, and every standard you refused to compromise.

We don't always get to control the end of our public story — councils change, politics shift, and loyalties fade. But we do control how we carry ourselves through it all. The courage to serve with integrity is not rewarded with fanfare; it's rewarded with peace of mind, with knowing you never became what you fought against.

So, when your career winds down, or when you face the next difficult season, remember this:

The measure of leadership isn't how much power you hold — it's how much truth you can stand to tell.

And if you've done that, even once, you've already succeeded.

— Charles A. Montoya

Acknowledgment

To my father—

Thank you for shaping the foundation of who I am.

You taught me early on the meaning of work ethic, responsibility, and standing up for what is right—even when it's hard, even when you're standing alone. Your quiet strength, your presence, and the example you set in how to live as a man, a father, and a leader have stayed with me through every chapter of my life and every test of my career.

When I became challenged—mentally, emotionally, and professionally—you were there. When I felt isolated, betrayed, and depressed, you were the one who stood by me.

You didn't run. You didn't flinch.

You reminded me that perseverance isn't just something we teach—it's something we live.

You were my first best friend, and you still are.

And when I found myself in the darkest moments of my life—facing medical crises, near death, and a world of uncertainty—you didn't falter.

You somehow found the strength not just to support me, but to push me harder, speak life into me, and pull me forward when others, including doctors, had given up.

In those moments, when I had nothing left, you gave me enough belief—enough force of will—to carry me through.

This book, these words, and the career they reflect would never have existed without you.

Thank you for being my first teacher, my constant compass, and the strongest man I know.

With unshakable love and eternal gratitude,

Your son, Charles

One Last Acknowledgment

To John Pazour –

My longtime mentor and the first city manager that I had, who taught me about integrity, self-assessment, self-preservation, and dignity. How to hold your head high in the tumultuous world of government that we work in.

Thank you for all your knowledge and guidance and for setting me on the right path.

Charles